Decorative & Ornamental
Scroll Saw Patterns

Patrick Spielman & Dirk Boelman

Sterling Publishing Co., Inc.
New York

ACKNOWLEDGMENTS

The authors express their sincere appreciation and gratitude to Karen Boelman and Julie Kiehnau for their expert scroll sawing of the many sample projects, and thanks, too, to Theresa Bezdecny and Denise LaHaye for their beautiful decorative painting of projects.

Library of Congress Cataloging-in-Publication Data

Spielman, Patrick E.
    Decorative & ornamental scroll saw patterns / Patrick Spielman
& Dirk Boelman.
        p. cm.
    Includes index.
    ISBN 0-8069-4236-3
        1. Jig saws.   2. Woodwork--Patterns.   I. Title.   II. Title: Decorative
    and ornamental scroll saw patterns. III. Boelman, Dirk.
    TT186.S6653 2000
    745.51'3 21 dc21   99-043497

Designed by Judy Morgan
Edited by Rodman P. Neumann

Every effort has been made to ensure that all the information in the book is accurate. However, due to differing conditions, tools, and individual skills, the publisher cannot be responsible for any injuries, losses, and other damages which may result from the use of the information in this book.

1 3 5 7 9 10 8 6 4 2

Published by Sterling Publishing Company, Inc.
387 Park Avenue South, New York, N.Y. 10016
© 2000 by Patrick Spielman and Dirk Boelman
Distributed in Canada by Sterling Publishing
c/o Canadian Manda Group, One Atlantic Avenue, Suite 105
Toronto, Ontario, Canada M6K 3E7
Distributed in Great Britain and Europe by Cassell PLC
Wellington House, 125 Strand, London WC2R 0BB, England
Distributed in Australia by Capricorn Link (Australia) Pty Ltd.
P.O. Box 6651, Baulkham Hills, Business Centre, NSW 2153, Australia
Printed in China
All rights reserved

Sterling ISBN 0-8069-4236-3

CONTENTS

PREFACE

Making ornaments and decorative items for the home is an extremely popular activity in all craft areas, including stitchery, ceramics, paper crafts, painting, and all forms of woodworking. Every fall, newsstands overflow with special-edition magazines dedicated entirely to ornament making for each of these popular craft areas. Ornaments are typically small, fun, easy-to-make projects for personal use, for gifts, or as objects to sell. Scroll-sawn ornaments sell well year round.

This book provides the largest and finest selection available anywhere of ornamental and decorative patterns and projects for scroll-saw cutting. Each and every design is the creation of the co-author, Dirk Boelman, America's leading scroll-saw pattern designer. His designs and artwork have appeared in many of my previous scroll saw books, and they regularly grace the pages of *Creative Wood Works and Crafts* magazine as well as the magazine's annual special-edition publication, "Wood Ornaments."

Here, with Dirk's designs and artwork presented in color, we have established a new standard in scroll-saw pattern presentation. The book contains well over 100 project variations and provides something for everyone: from hanging ornaments and three-dimensional centerpieces to doll furniture and elegant jewelry. The designs have great market potential for those woodworkers wanting to sell their work in shops and at craft fairs. Dirk and I encourage the use of these patterns for this activity. We do, however, stipulate herewith that the designs are not permitted to be made by laser, water jet, CNC routers, engravers, or any other forms of high-volume production equipment. Scrollers are permitted to make any number of projects they wish, as long as they are hand-cut using conventional scroll saws. Incidentally, copying patterns to give, trade, or sell is a violation of copyright.

This book is intended for everyone who possesses basic scroll-sawing and woodworking skills. Rather than elaborate on or repeat this information, we prefer to use this space to provide you with more patterns and more useful information. If you are new to scrolling, we recommend a book such as *Scroll Saw Basics*, also published by STERLING PUBLISHING CO.

Where special techniques are required to complete a project, that information will be incorporated into the presentation of the project with text, line drawings, or photographs. We do offer a few general tips and suggestions that are intended to alert you to more options and better use of the patterns.

—Patrick Spielman

TIPS & SUGGESTIONS

Material Choices

Select quality hardwood plywoods when thin stock is specified and where strength is important. Highly detailed fretwork and toys will be more durable if cut from plywood. All plans and patterns are drawn in U.S. (Imperial) dimensions. Therefore, slight adjustments must be made to the patterns when using materials of metric sizes. (Refer to the section on "Metric Conversion" on page 126, before the Index.) This is especially true when you are making three-dimensional projects with halved joints. Baltic birch plywood 6mm in thickness, for example, is close to ¼" but it is actually slightly thinner.

Use solid hardwoods for making household accessories and all projects that will look better without plywood edges. Consider using plastics, paper, metal, and other materials to obtain visual variety using the same pattern.

Solid white acrylic plastic with a blue translucent backer makes a striking ornament. Clear silicon adhesive was used.

Pattern Sizes

The patterns provided are all full size and ready for use. To obtain the fullest possible use of them, consider enlarging them substantially to create yard art and exterior home decorations. Reduce the same pattern to create interesting miniatures.

Finishes

As a general rule, we suggest avoiding high-gloss finishes on natural wood and fretwork pieces. Use acrylics on pieces you intend to paint

Bright gold aerosol finish gives ⅛″ Baltic birch a brilliant metallic look. (See photo on page 14.)

because of their quick-drying quality and easy water cleanup. Consider using the many specialty spray finishes available; not only is their application very convenient but you can also easily create very dramatic effects. Specialty sprays are available in a variety of finishes including flock, crackle, faux stone, marble, and metallic.

Decorative Appearance

You'll notice that many projects feature decorative "add-ons" such as leather, bright-colored cords, ribbons, beads, feathers, clock and photo inserts, and decorative hardware. Most of these items are readily available at craft and hobby shops, leather working stores, or by mail order. Should you have difficulty finding a particular item, please write us in care of the publisher or simply substitute as best you can.

Preparation for an easy-to-achieve patina finish on ⅛″ plywood. First the project is coated with a clear sealer followed with a coat or two of water-based bronze or copper liquid metal, as shown here.

A sponge application of the patina solution provides an unpatterned contrast that oxidizes the metallic substrate. This creates a remarkable resemblance to real aged metal. (See the patina-finished projects on pages 45, 51, and 52.)

PATTERN CATEGORIES

1 HANGING FLAT ORNAMENTS

Ornaments can be made from a variety of materials, but most common is plywood ¹⁄₃₂" to ¼" thick.

Tip

Hang your completed ornaments with festive-colored ribbons, cords, or strings . . . and decorate them with beads, bells, and other holiday trim.

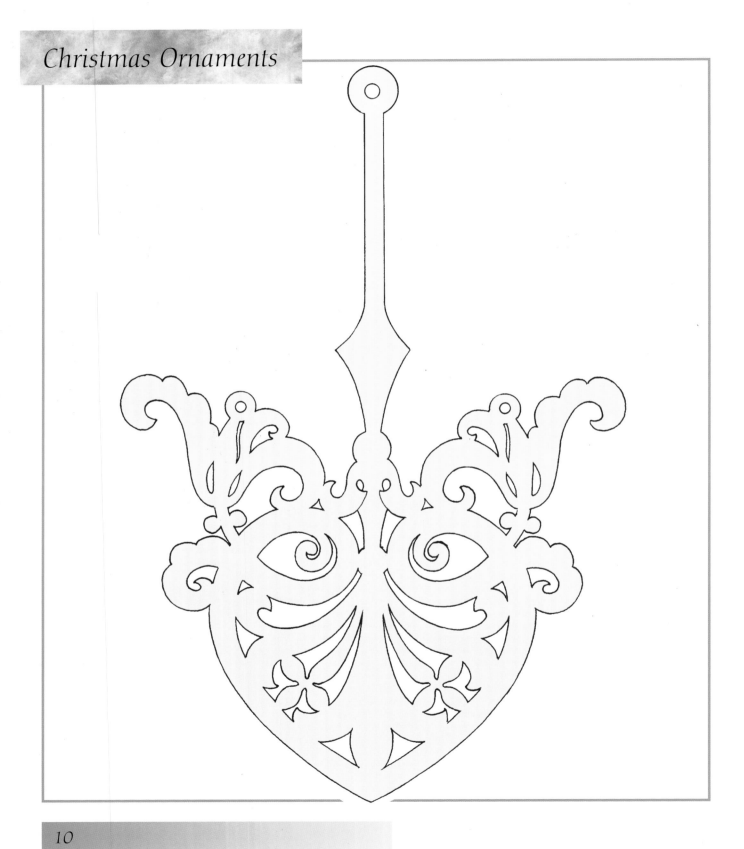

Painted finish.

This can be made from material of your choice. It looks great in natural wood tones, or can be stained or painted as desired. Acrylic plastic also works well.

Hang your completed ornaments with festive-colored ribbons or string and decorate them with beads, bells, and other holiday trim.

Hang it with festive-colored ribbons/string and adorn it with beads, bells, and other holiday trim.

⅛" Baltic birch with sprayed-on metallic finish.

Painted finish
with glitter.

Make them from aromatic cedar and hang them in your closet-to keep the real bugs away!

2 HANGING 3-D ORNAMENTS

3-D Ornaments, ⅛" painted plywood.

3-D ORNAMENTS are designed to be made from ⅛" thick material.

They use a half-joint to fasten sections together. Since the actual thickness of materials will vary, you may need to adjust the width of the joint on the patterns. Lay your materials on edge over the slotted areas and trace their outline on the pattern. Saw slightly to the inside edges of your newly drawn pattern lines; sand or file to fit.

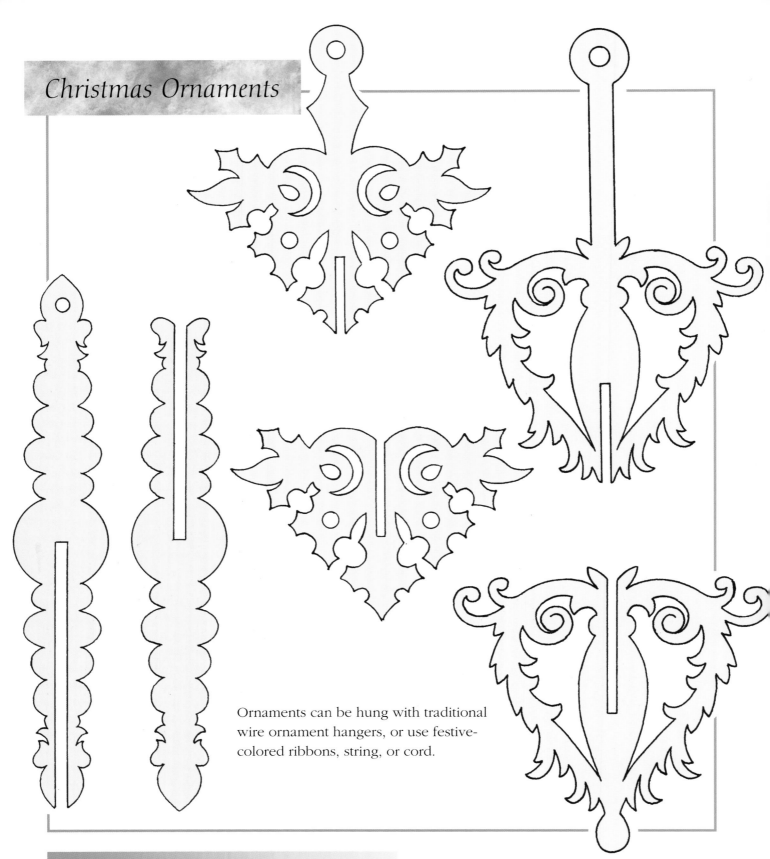

Ornaments can be hung with traditional wire ornament hangers, or use festive-colored ribbons, string, or cord.

Make from ⅛" thick material.

These designs utilize a half-joint to give them a 3-D appearance. Adjust the width of the opening to match up with the actual thickness of the materials you are using, by placing it on edge on the pattern, and tracing its outline. Then saw to the inside edge of the lines.

3

DECORATIVE BIRDS

Above: Suspend your completed birds from a hoop or branch. Right: Typical birds, unassembled and unpainted.

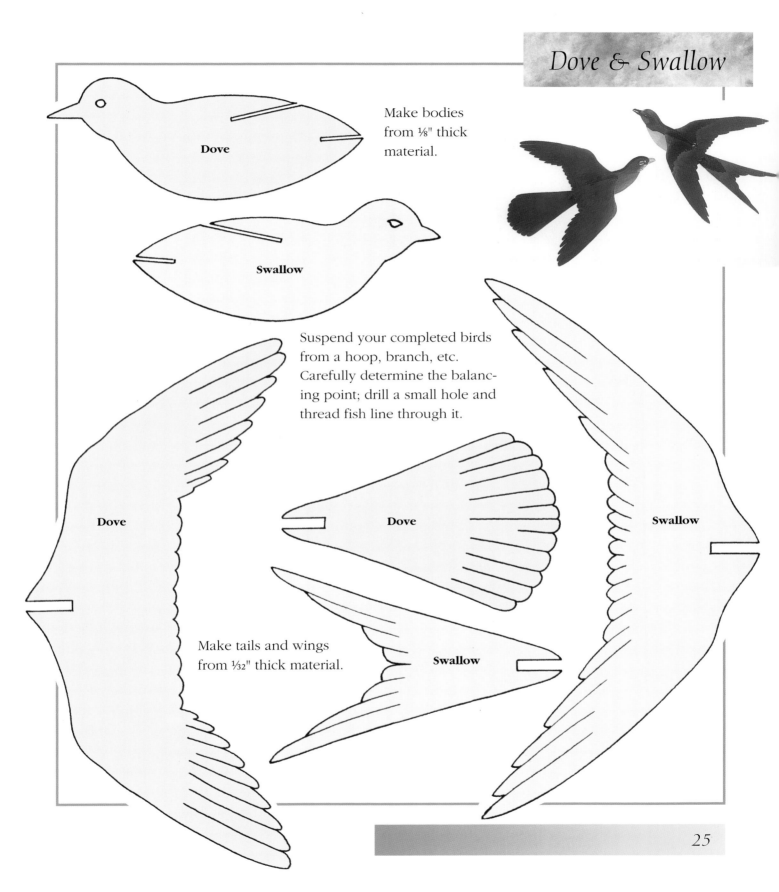

Dove

Swallow

Make bodies from ⅛" thick material.

Suspend your completed birds from a hoop, branch, etc. Carefully determine the balancing point; drill a small hole and thread fish line through it.

Dove

Dove

Swallow

Swallow

Make tails and wings from ⅟₃₂" thick material.

Cardinal & Blue Jay

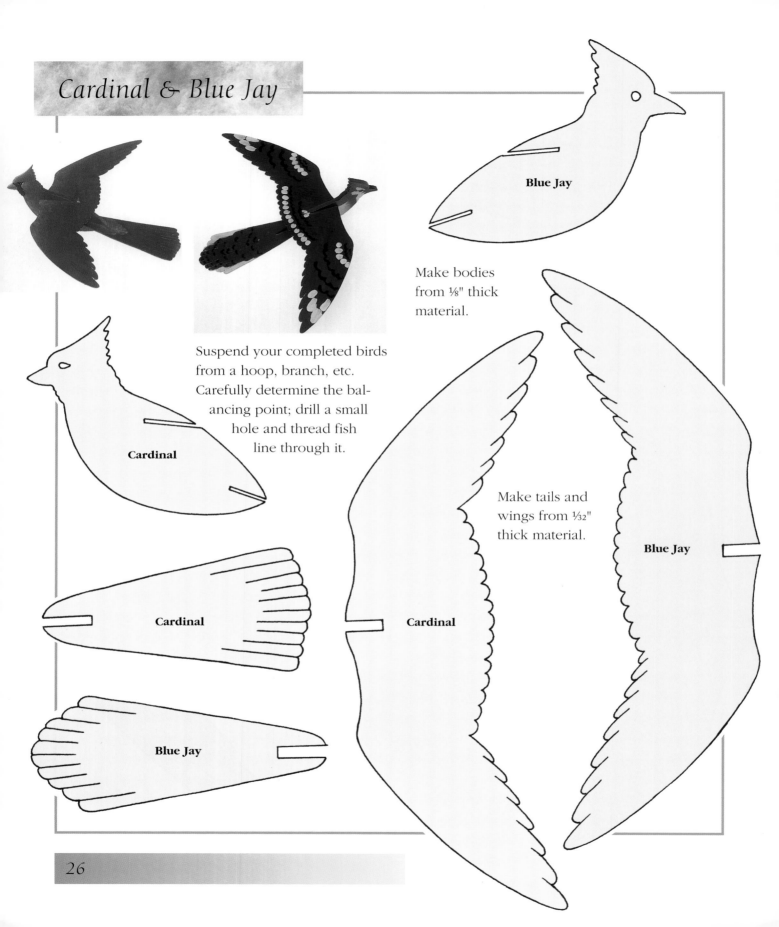

Blue Jay

Make bodies from ⅛" thick material.

Suspend your completed birds from a hoop, branch, etc. Carefully determine the balancing point; drill a small hole and thread fish line through it.

Cardinal

Make tails and wings from 1/32" thick material.

Cardinal

Blue Jay

Cardinal

Blue Jay

Hummingbird

Hummingbird

Hummingbird

Make bodies from ⅛" thick material.

Hang the bird with fish line.

Suspend your completed birds from a hoop, branch, etc. Carefully determine the balancing point; drill a small hole and thread fish line through it.

Robin

Robin

Robin

Make tails and wings from ⅟₃₂" thick material.

4 TABLETOP DECORATIONS

Santa's sleigh. Parts can be stack-cut, except for his initials ("SC"), which must be cut individually.

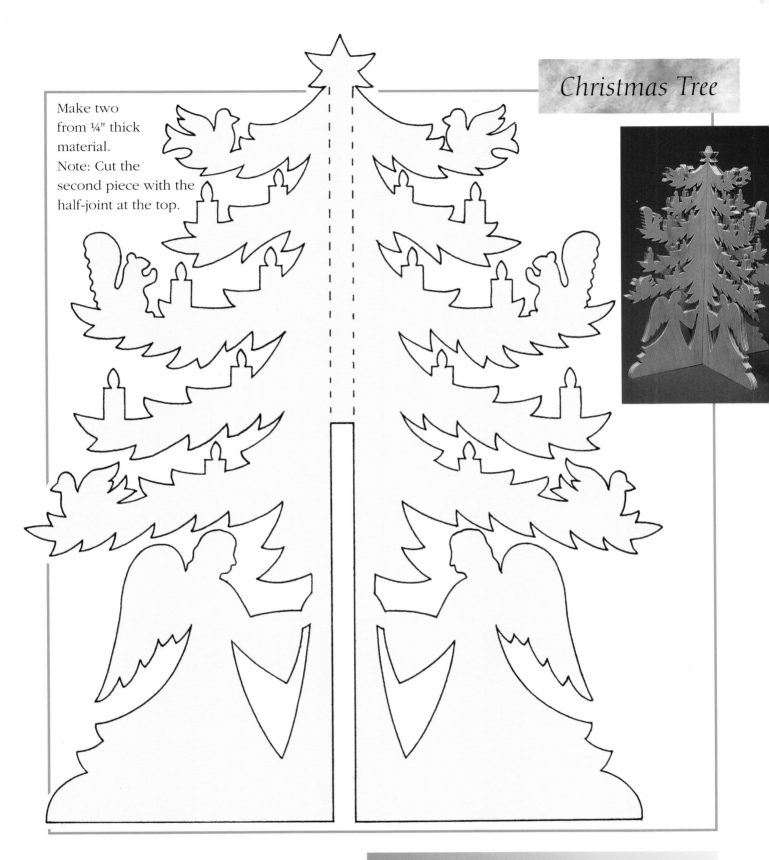

Make two
from ¼" thick
material.
Note: Cut the
second piece with the
half-joint at the top.

Christmas Tree

Enlarge the pattern 200 percent
on a photocopy machine.

A

EDGE OF BASE

TOP OF BASE

Make the base from ¾" thick material.

Bevel or shape edges as desired.
(We chose a 30 degree bevel.)

B

Make from ¾" thick material.

A

B

Join patterns along line A–B.

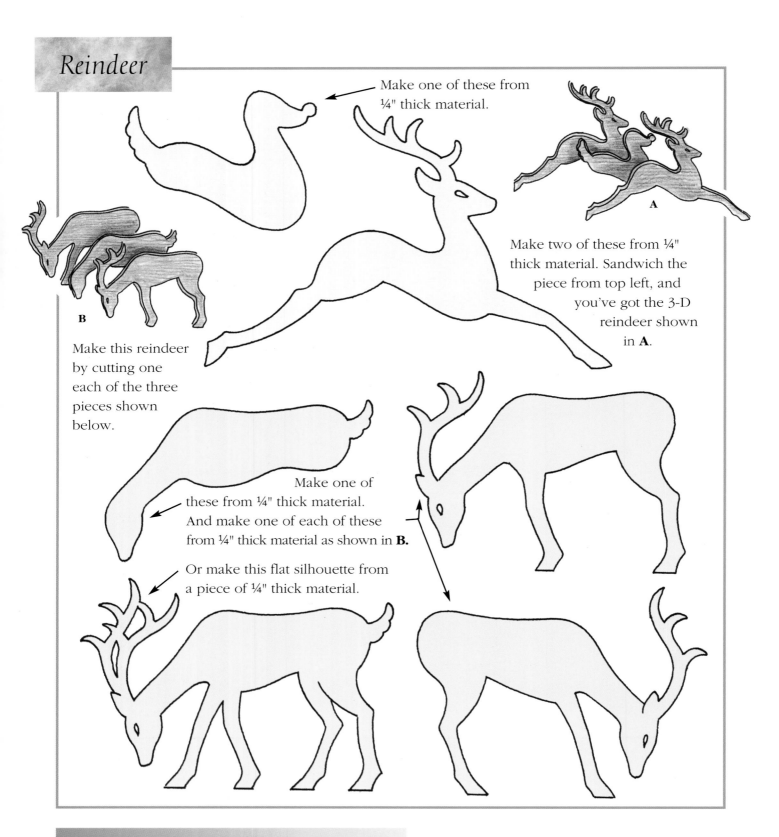

Make one of these from ¼" thick material.

Make two of these from ¼" thick material. Sandwich the piece from top left, and you've got the 3-D reindeer shown in **A**.

A

B

Make this reindeer by cutting one each of the three pieces shown below.

Make one of these from ¼" thick material. And make one of each of these from ¼" thick material as shown in **B**.

Or make this flat silhouette from a piece of ¼" thick material.

Make one of each of these three parts to create the reindeer shown in **C**.

C

Or just make this silhouette from one piece of ¼" thick material.

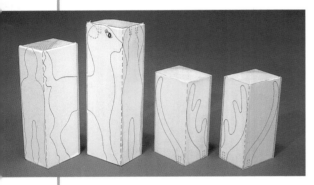

Blocks with reindeer body and antler patterns applied to two surfaces ready for compound sawing. Note: Each reindeer body is sawn from two blocks.

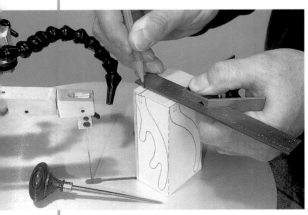

Locate antler dowel holes.

REINDEER EARS
Make from ⅛" thick material.

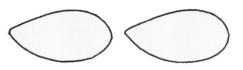

THE DEER are compound-sawn from 1⁷⁄₁₆" × 2" material. Before sawing, mark and drill the two ⅛" diameter holes in the top of the reindeer's head to insert dowels to attach the antlers.

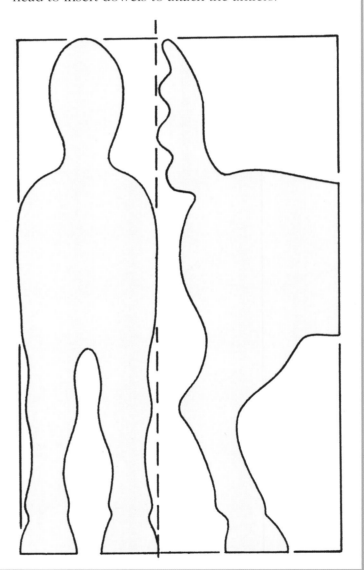

After completing compound-sawing, reassemble the pieces; hold them together with masking tape; tilt scroll saw table 7 degrees and saw along lines to roughly shape a snout.

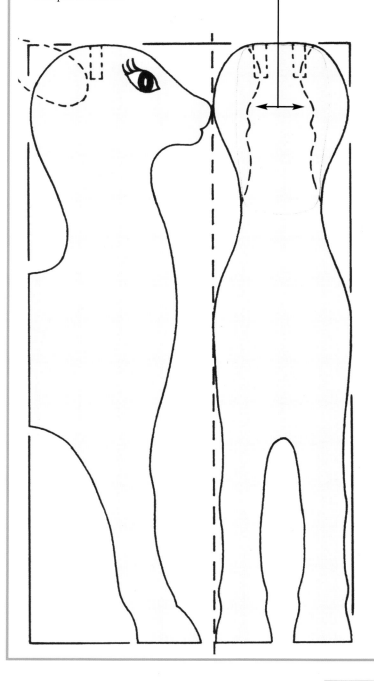

Drill the holes in the antler pieces and the head piece of the body before compound-sawing the rough shapes.

The two halves of each body are glued as shown. The corners are then rounded over with power rotary tools, files, abrasives, or by other means. Note: All reindeer and Santa's sleigh are glued to a board base.

Santa's 3-D Reindeer

ANTLERS are also compound-sawn from 1⁷⁄₁₆" x 2" material. Before sawing, locate and drill the ⅛" diameter holes for the dowels to attach the antlers to the reindeers' heads.

Cut ⅝" lengths of ⅛" diameter dowel to attach each antler.

Making one of the "first cuts" on an antler piece.

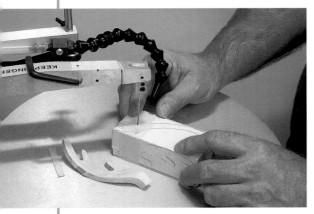

Making the "second cut" on the same antler piece. Note the sample antler piece sawn out and partly shaped with its corners rounded.

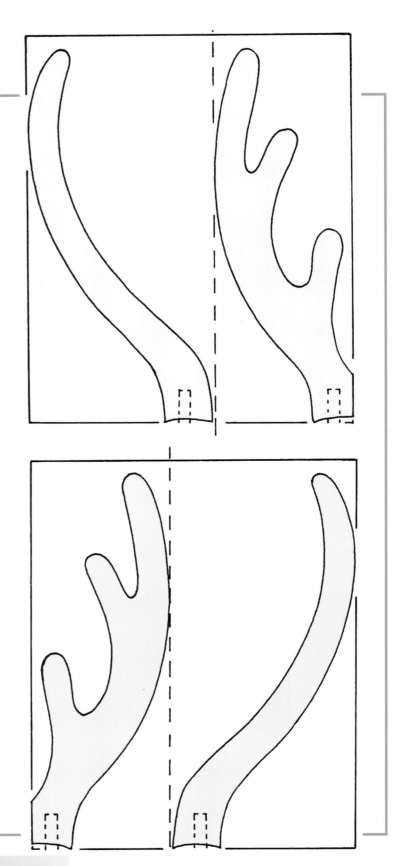

RUNNERS
Make two from ¾" thick stock.

Make two **SIDE PANELS** from ½" thick material. Note that the two side panels can be stack-cut, except for Santa's initials ("SC"), which must be cut individually in order that they read correctly when the sides are in place facing out.

BOTTOM
Make from ½" thick material.

SIDE VIEW OF BOTTOM PANEL. Bevel front edge 15 degrees.

20-degree bevel.

EDGE VIEW OF SEAT

SEAT SUPPORT
Make from ½" thick material.

SEAT
Make from ¼" thick material. Bevel the back edge 20 degrees, as shown on the edge view above.

Santa's sleigh. Parts can be stack-cut, except for his initials ("SC"), which must be cut individually.

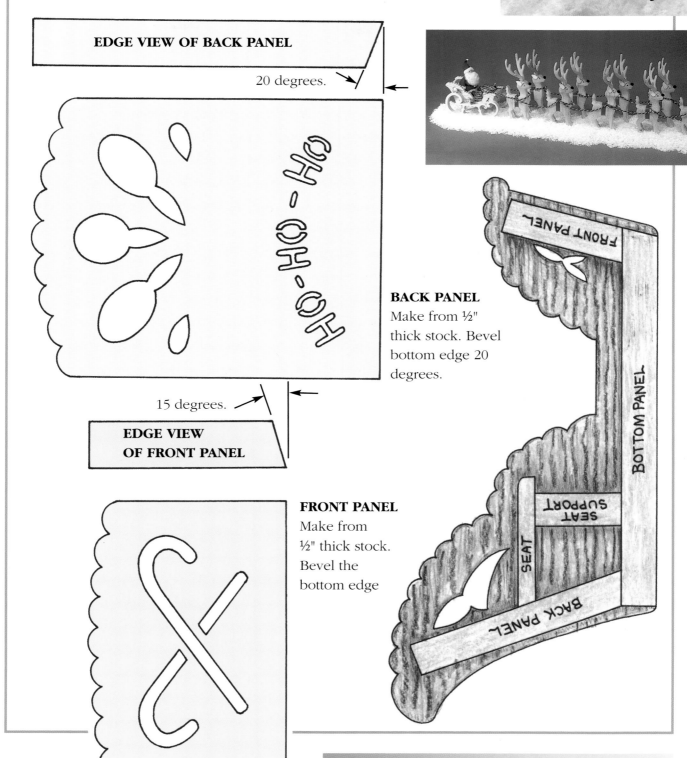

EDGE VIEW OF BACK PANEL

20 degrees.

HO-HO-HO

15 degrees.

**EDGE VIEW
OF FRONT PANEL**

BACK PANEL
Make from ½"
thick stock. Bevel
bottom edge 20
degrees.

FRONT PANEL
Make from
½" thick stock.
Bevel the
bottom edge

FRONT PANEL

BOTTOM PANEL

SEAT SUPPORT

SEAT

BACK PANEL

5 ANGELS & RELIGIOUS ITEMS

The Angels of Joy and the Musical Angel.

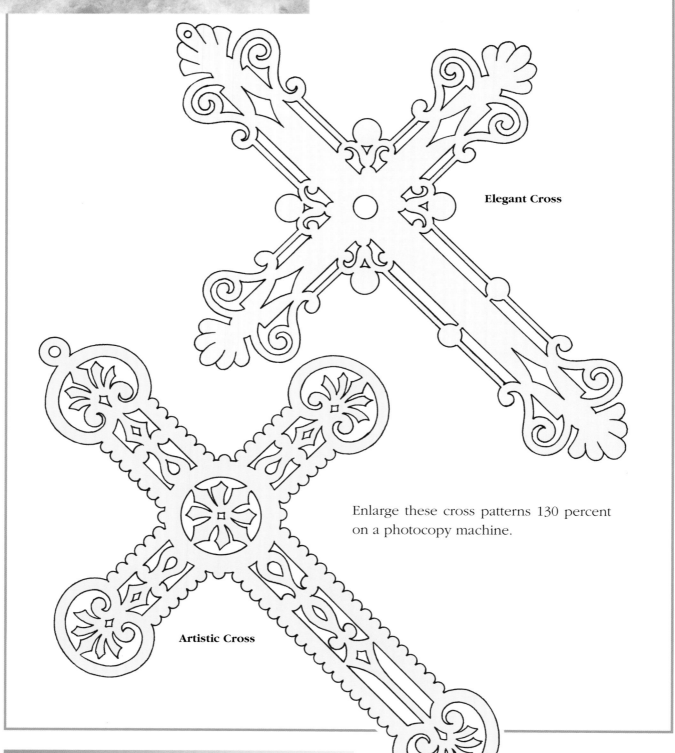

Elegant Cross

Enlarge these cross patterns 130 percent on a photocopy machine.

Artistic Cross

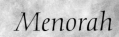

Menorah

This has a
patina finish to
look like metal.

Cut from ⅛" plywood.

Same lettering pattern cut from ¾" stock makes a table decoration.

6 SOUTHWEST DESIGNS

These designs lend themselves to display in windows, as wall hanging,s or. perhaps, as neclaces. Note that variations include using real feathers as well as the scroll-cut wooden ones.

7 DECORATIVE WALL ART

The Clown works well as a wall hanging.

American Eagle

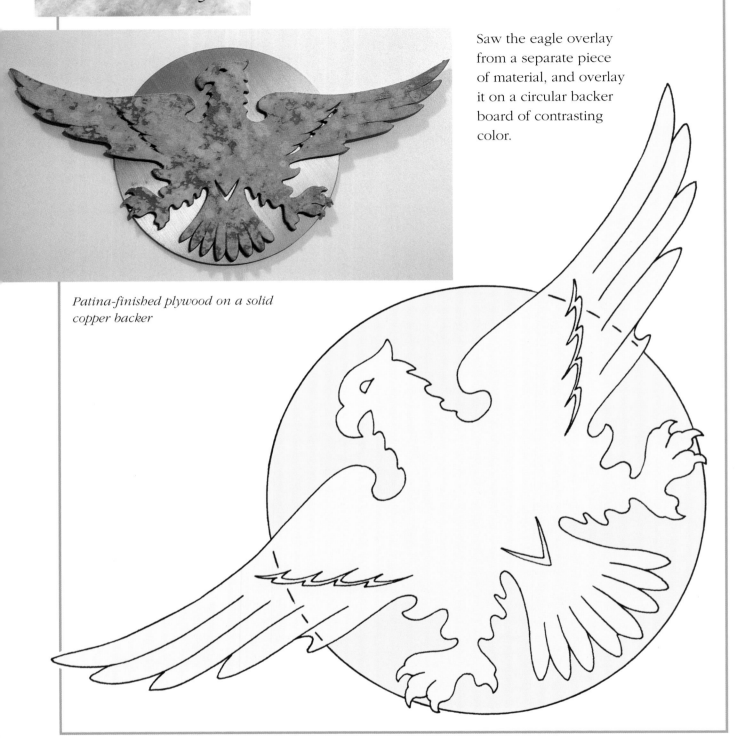

Saw the eagle overlay from a separate piece of material, and overlay it on a circular backer board of contrasting color.

Patina-finished plywood on a solid copper backer

Feline

Butterfly

Make various sizes of **BUTTERFLIES** from your favorite colors of wood, or paint and stain as desired. A few ideas include: making two at a time, and sandwiching them together with thin plastic sheet between, with cutout areas decorated with bright-colored markers; or you might eliminate all of the interior cutouts and just paint the spots on your butterflies; or make them from colored acrylic plastic. Be creative!

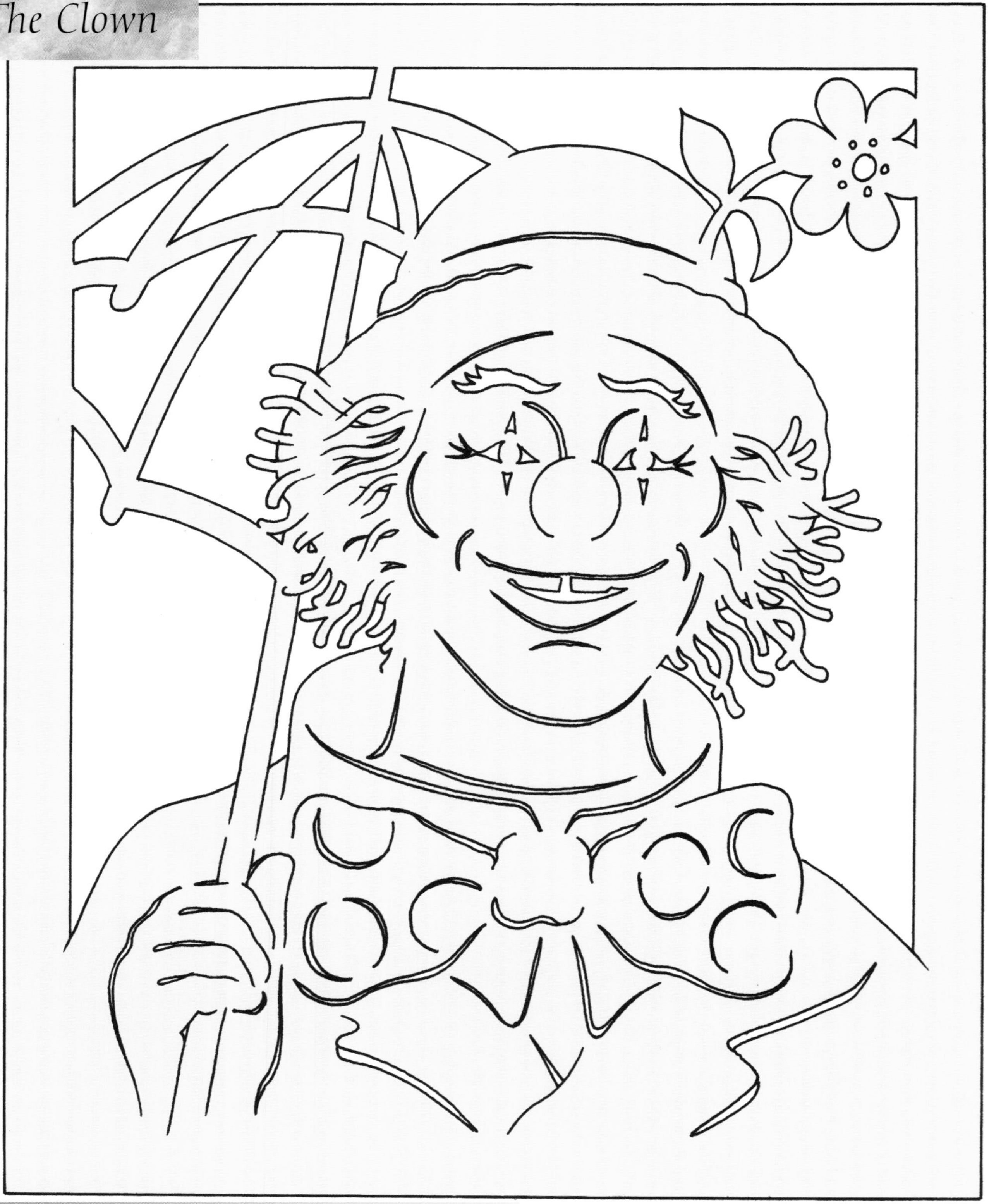

8 CLOCKS

The Thompson table clock makes a handsome standing clock.

Make from ¼" thick material.

The Thompson table clock is designed to hold a 2" diameter clock insert. (Modify the size of the mounting hole as needed, to fit your insert.)

$1\frac{13}{16}$

$1\frac{3}{8}$

Location of legs

The Thompson Table Clock

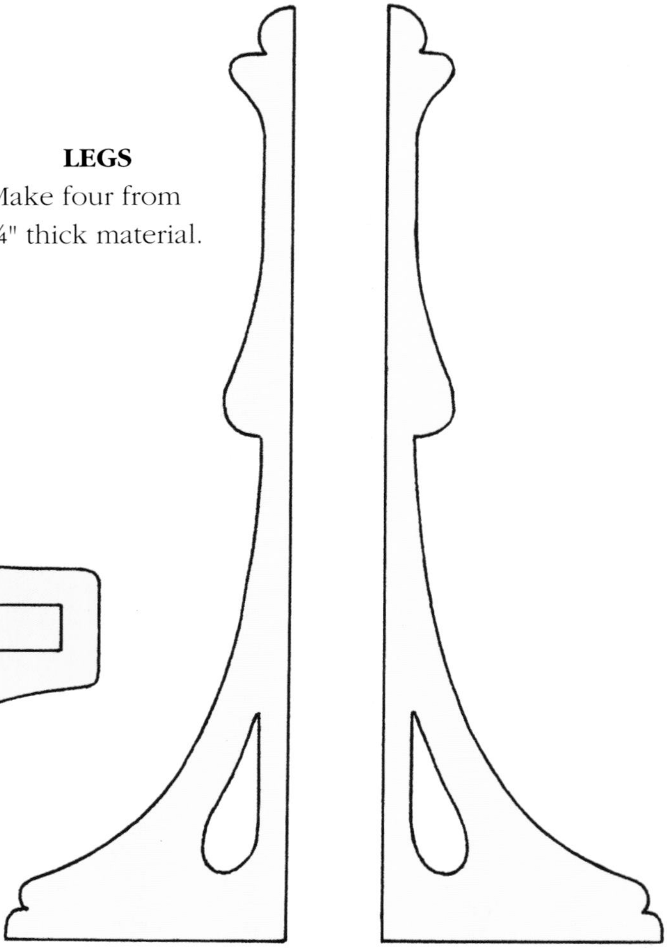

LEGS
Make four from
¼" thick material.

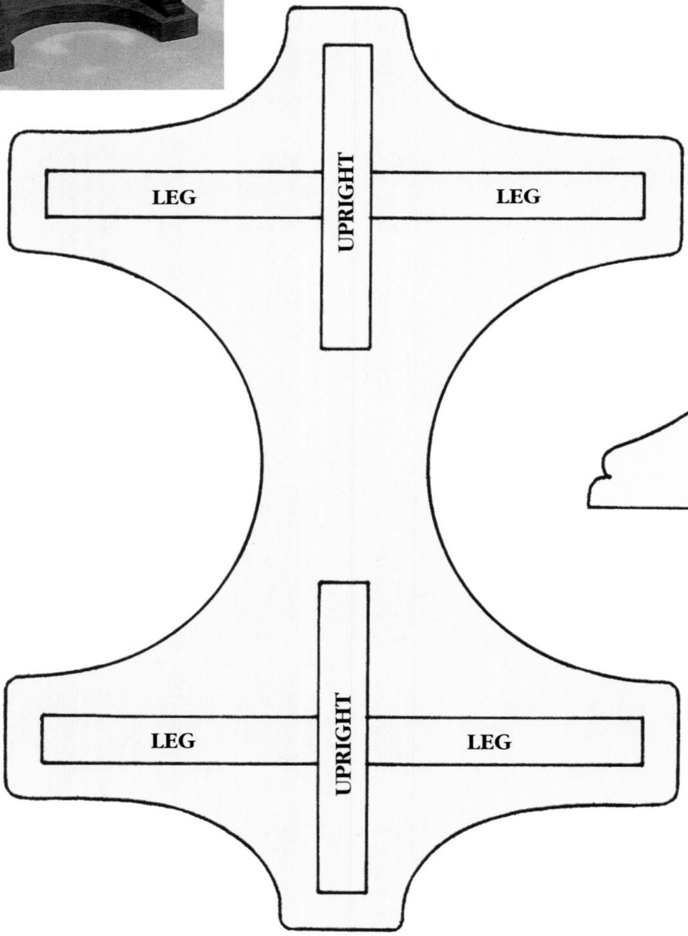

BASE
Make from ¼" thick material.

NOTE: Locations are shown where parts attach to the base. Do not cut out these areas.

LEG

UPRIGHT

LEG

LEG

UPRIGHT

LEG

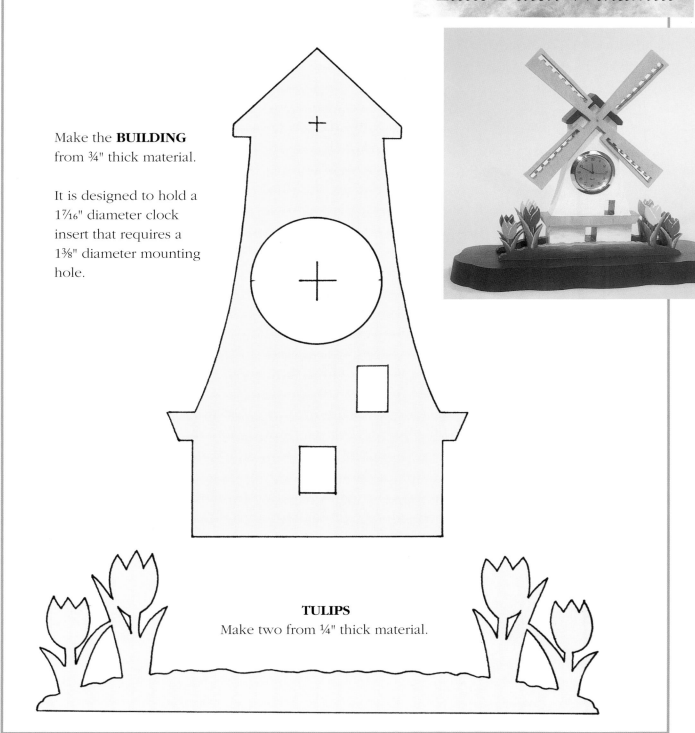

Make the **BUILDING**
from ¾" thick material.

It is designed to hold a
1⁷⁄₁₆" diameter clock
insert that requires a
1³⁄₈" diameter mounting
hole.

TULIPS
Make two from ¼" thick material.

Little Dutch Windmill

BLADES

Make from ¼" thick material.

Drill a small hole in the center to attach to the building with a small nail or brad.

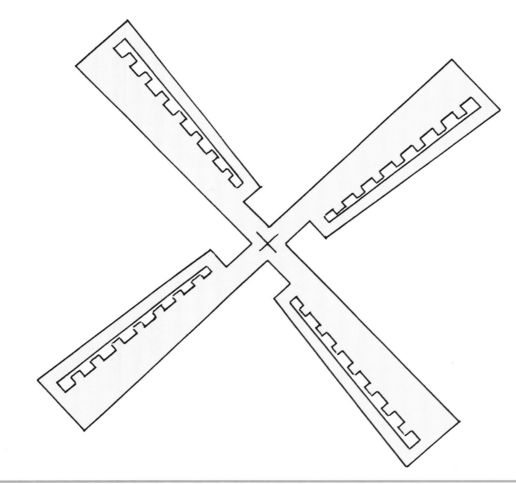

TULIPS

BUILDING

TULIPS

BASE

Make from ¾" thick material.

The edge can be bevel-sawn at 10 degrees to 15 degrees as desired.

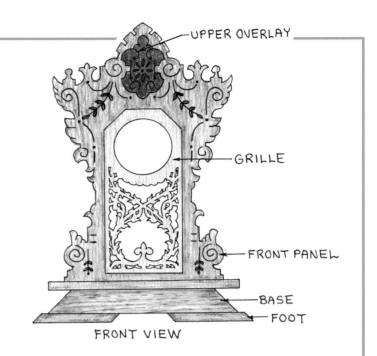

UPPER OVERLAY

GRILLE

FRONT PANEL

BASE

FOOT

FRONT VIEW

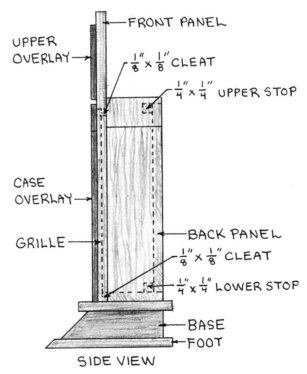

FRONT PANEL

UPPER OVERLAY

$\frac{1}{8}" \times \frac{1}{8}"$ CLEAT

$\frac{1}{4}" \times \frac{1}{4}"$ UPPER STOP

CASE OVERLAY

GRILLE

BACK PANEL

$\frac{1}{8}" \times \frac{1}{8}"$ CLEAT

$\frac{1}{4}" \times \frac{1}{4}"$ LOWER STOP

BASE

FOOT

SIDE VIEW

FRONT PANEL
Make from ¼" thick material.

OVERLAY
Make from ⅛" thick material.

GRILLE
Make from ⅛" thick material.

The grille of this kitchen clock is designed to hold a 1⁷⁄₁₆" diameter clock insert that requires a 1⅜" diameter mounting hole.

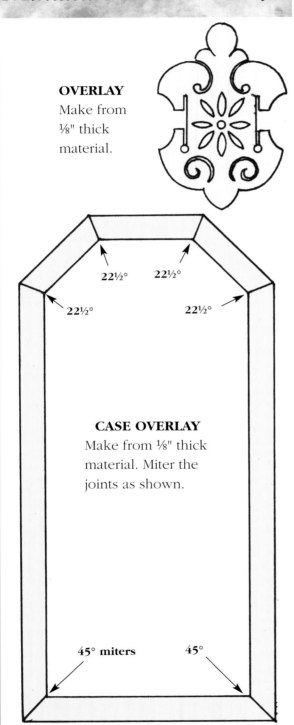

22½°   22½°

22½°   22½°

CASE OVERLAY
Make from ⅛" thick material. Miter the joints as shown.

45° miters   45°

TOP

Make from ¼" thick stock.

Bevel ends at 22½ degrees.

CLOCK CASE

Made from six pieces of ¼" thick material.

SLOPES. Make two from ¼" thick stock. Bevel top and bottom ends at 22½ degrees.

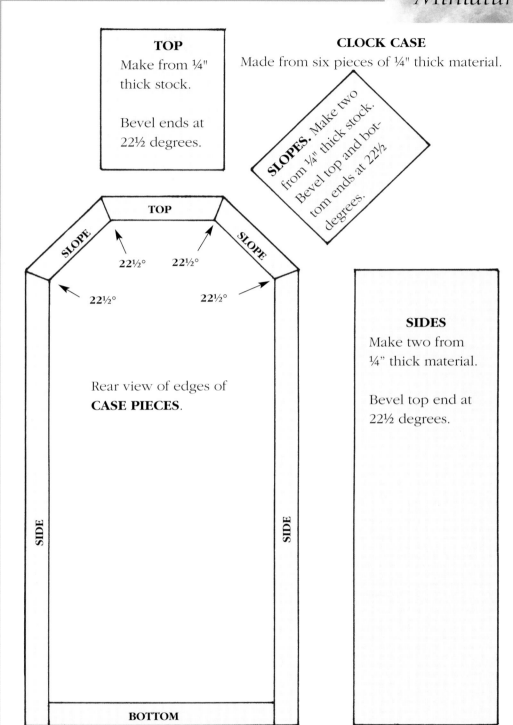

SLOPE

TOP

SLOPE

22½° 22½°

22½° 22½°

Rear view of edges of **CASE PIECES**.

SIDE

SIDE

BOTTOM

SIDES

Make two from ¼" thick material.

Bevel top end at 22½ degrees.

This clock is designed to utilize a miniature pendulum drive unit, similar to the illustration at left. Follow manufacturer's instructions to install. Attach to the back panel, centered on the location indicated on the pattern. Trim the pendulum rod to the desired length.

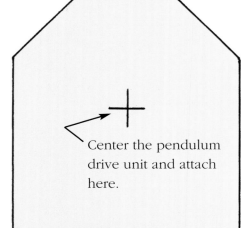

Center the pendulum drive unit and attach here.

BACK PANEL
Make from ¼" thick stock.

Refer to the side view on page 68, which shows the installation of upper and lower stops inside the clock case. Make and install these stops to prevent the door from being pushed too far inside the clock case.

Make the back panel so that it can be removed for access to the movement. A knob can be fastened to the backside if desired.

TOP OF BASE
Make from ¼" thick material.

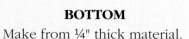

BOTTOM
Make from ¼" thick material.

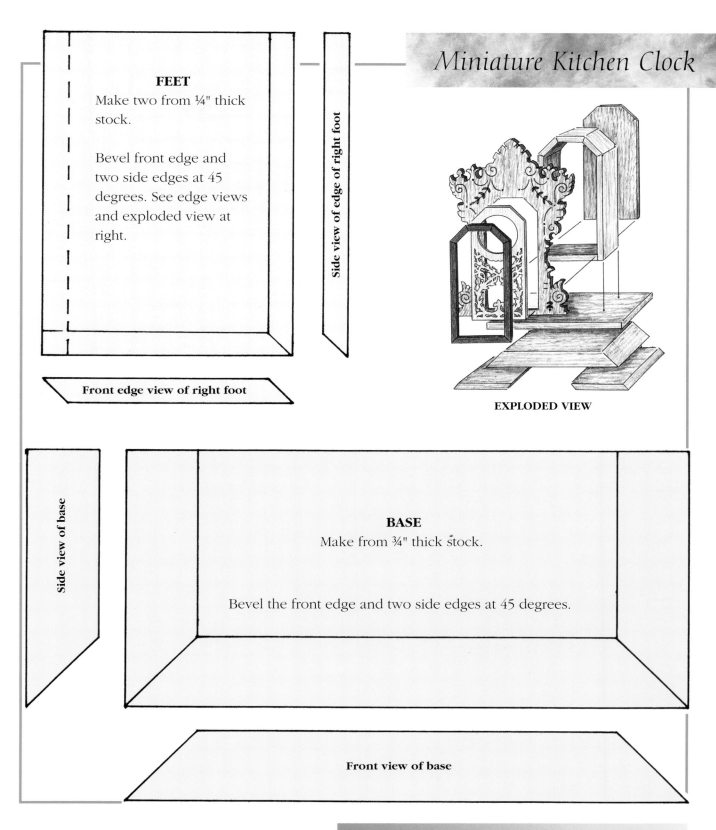

FEET

Make two from ¼" thick stock.

Bevel front edge and two side edges at 45 degrees. See edge views and exploded view at right.

Side view of edge of right foot

Front edge view of right foot

EXPLODED VIEW

BASE

Make from ¾" thick stock.

Bevel the front edge and two side edges at 45 degrees.

Side view of base

Front view of base

TOYS & DOLL FURNITURE

Victoriran Doll Chair and Table. The chair has an upholstered appearance by applying fabric-covered cardboard to the seat and back.

Traditional "Jumping Jack" figures are quick and easy to make from ¼" thick material.

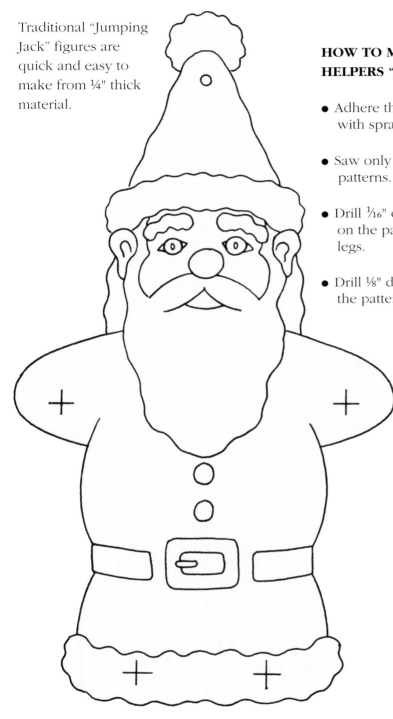

HOW TO MAKE THE SANTA & HELPERS "JUMPING JACK" TOYS

- Adhere the patterns to the wood with spray glue.

- Saw only on the outlines of the patterns.

- Drill ¹⁄₁₆" diameter holes at the dots on the patterns of the arms and legs.

- Drill ⅛" diameter holes at the +'s on the patterns

NOTE: Before assembly, paint all the parts as desired, then redrill holes to allow arms and legs to move freely.

- Also before assembly, loop strings through the arms and legs as shown in the drawing at the right. The strings need to be long enough to extend a few inches below the feet when assembled.

(The instructions are contined on pages 76 and 77 following.)

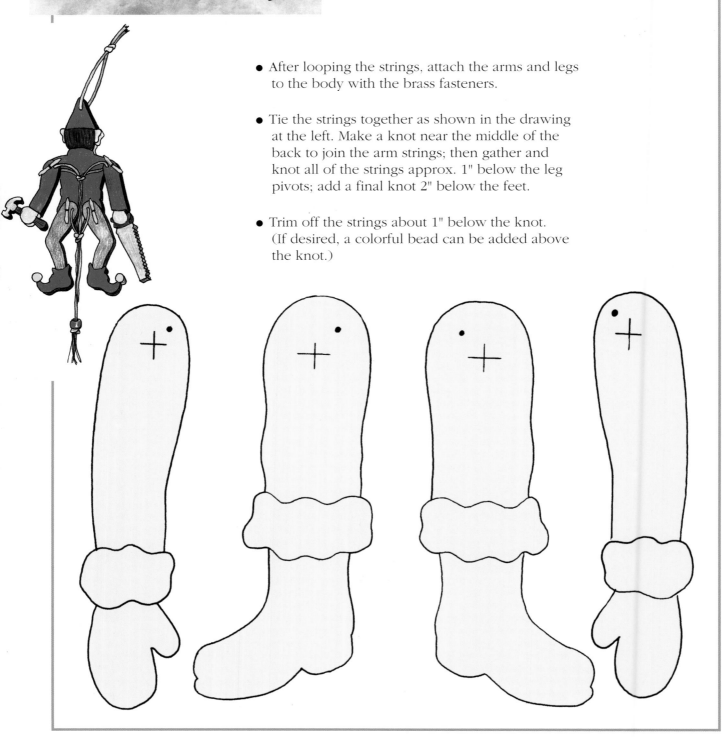

- After looping the strings, attach the arms and legs to the body with the brass fasteners.

- Tie the strings together as shown in the drawing at the left. Make a knot near the middle of the back to join the arm strings; then gather and knot all of the strings approx. 1" below the leg pivots; add a final knot 2" below the feet.

- Trim off the strings about 1" below the knot. (If desired, a colorful bead can be added above the knot.)

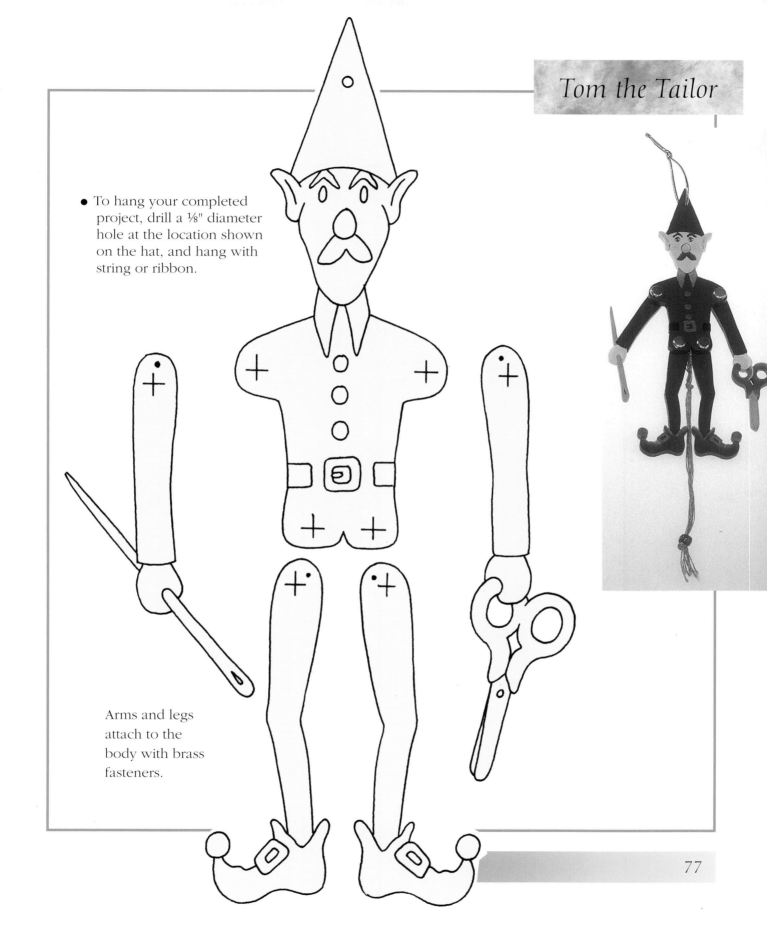

● To hang your completed project, drill a ⅛" diameter hole at the location shown on the hat, and hang with string or ribbon.

Arms and legs attach to the body with brass fasteners.

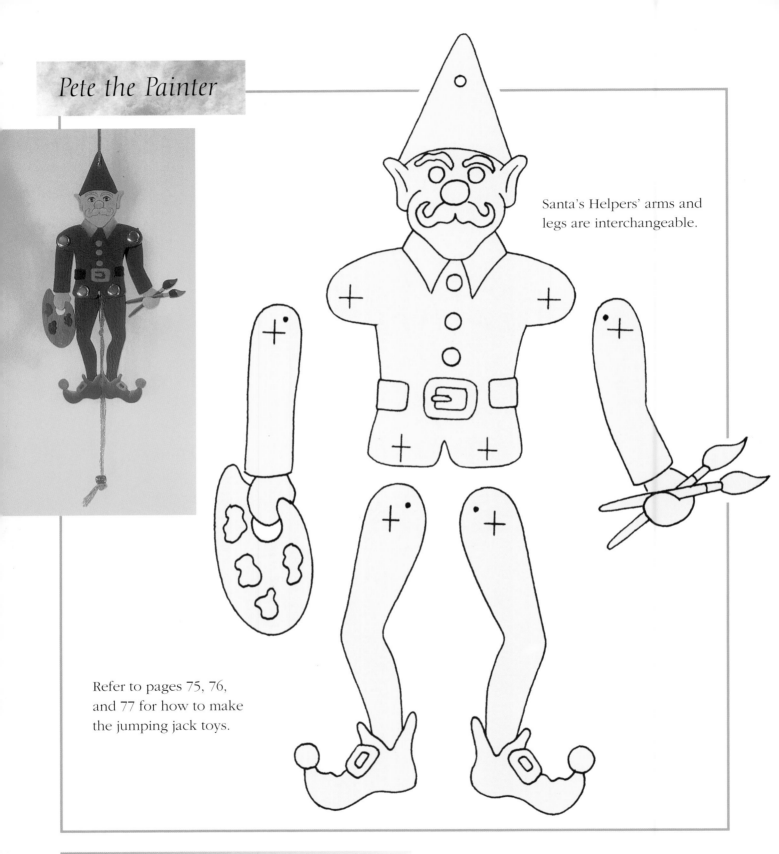

Pete the Painter

Santa's Helpers' arms and legs are interchangeable.

Refer to pages 75, 76, and 77 for how to make the jumping jack toys.

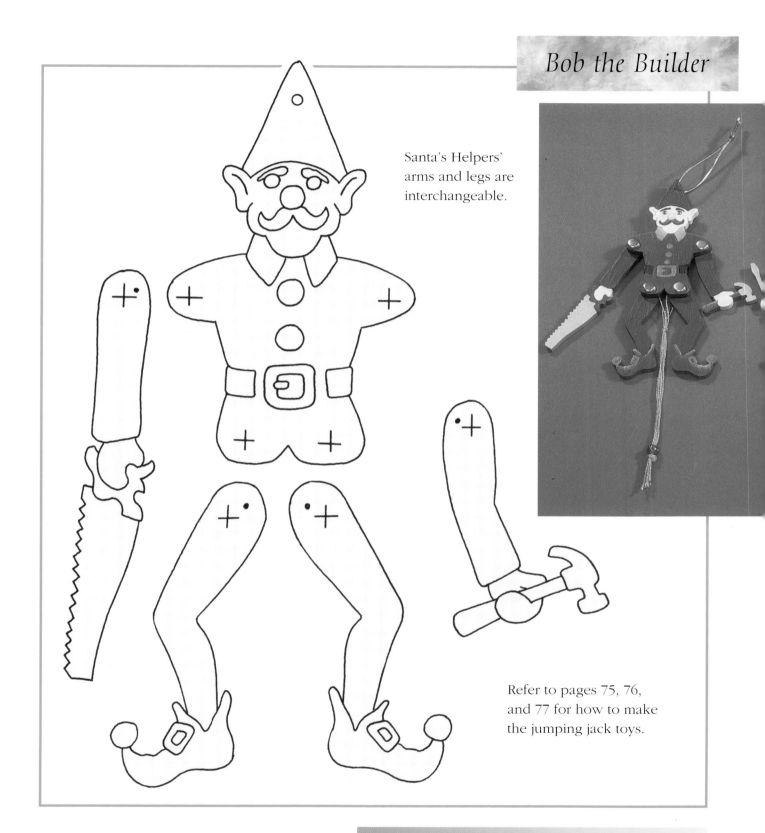

Santa's Helpers' arms and legs are interchangeable.

Refer to pages 75, 76, and 77 for how to make the jumping jack toys.

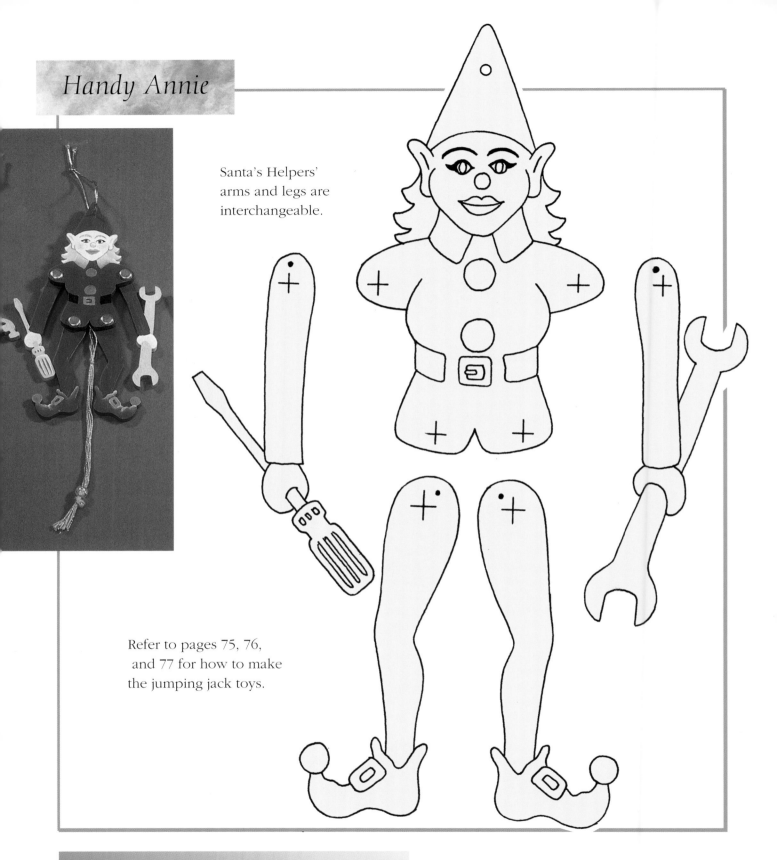

Handy Annie

Santa's Helpers'
arms and legs are
interchangeable.

Refer to pages 75, 76,
and 77 for how to make
the jumping jack toys.

CHAIR SIDES

Make from ¼" thick material.

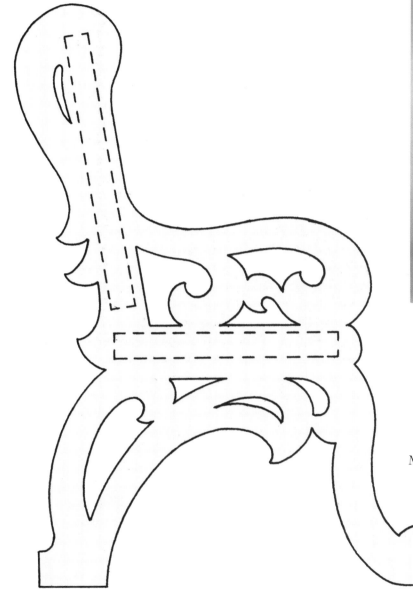

Make two sides for each chair.

Victorian Doll Chairs

BACK & SEAT

Make from ¼" thick material.

HOW TO MAKE THE CUSHIONS

Make seat and back cushions by cutting
a piece of cardboard to the size of the
dashed outlines shown on the patterns.

Cut pieces of fabric approx. ½" wider
and longer than the cardboard.

Wrap the fabric around the cardboard;
glue the fabric to back of cardboard.

Glue the cardboard and fabric assembly
in place onto chair.

TOP VIEW OF CHAIR BACK

Bevel edges 5 degrees.

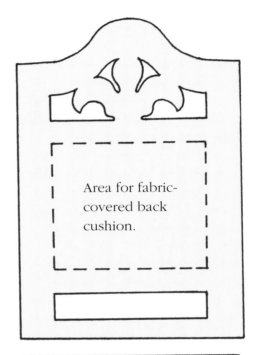

Area for fabric-covered back cushion.

Area for fabric-covered seat cushion.

ARM SECTIONS
Make two from ¼" thick material.

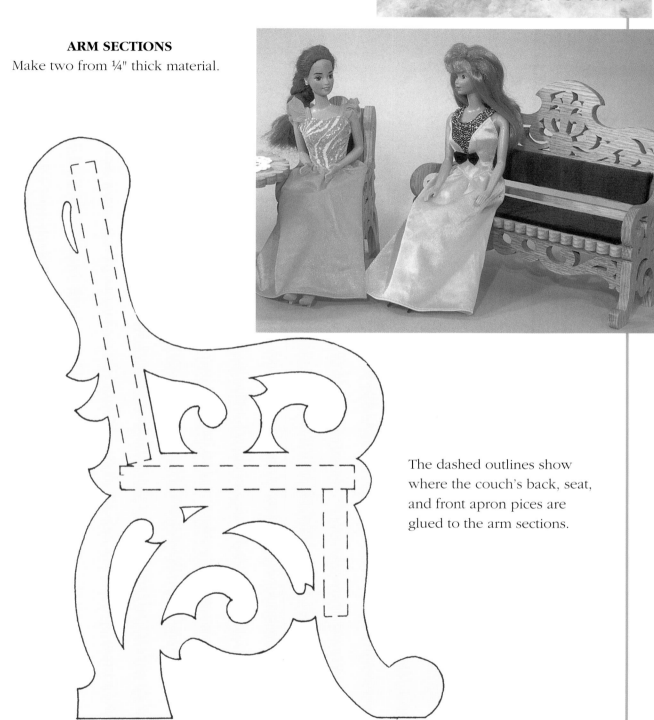

The dashed outlines show where the couch's back, seat, and front apron pices are glued to the arm sections.

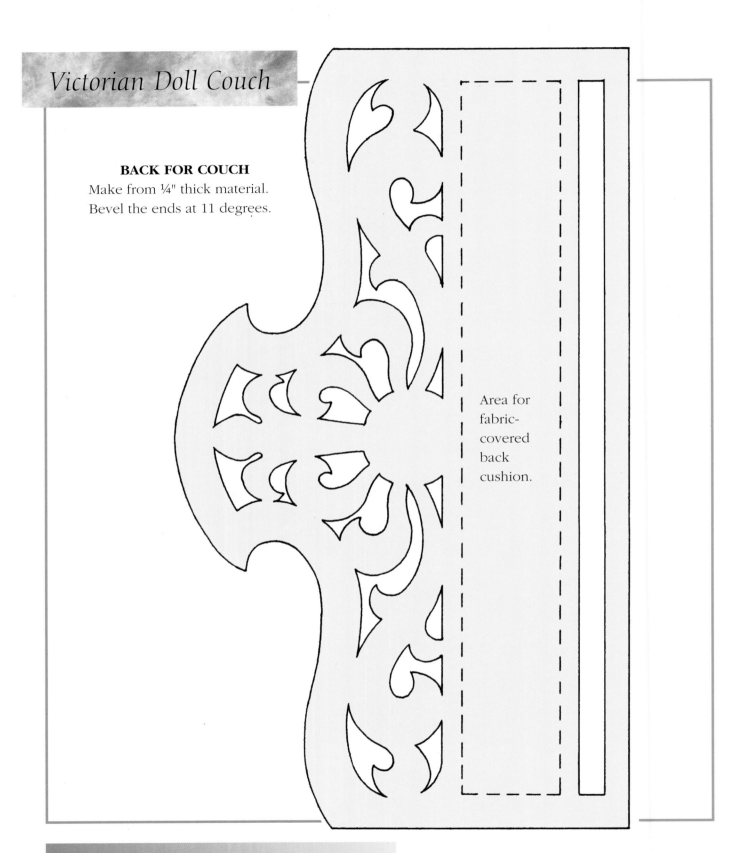

Victorian Doll Couch

BACK FOR COUCH

Make from ¼" thick material.
Bevel the ends at 11 degrees.

Area for
fabric-
covered
back
cushion.

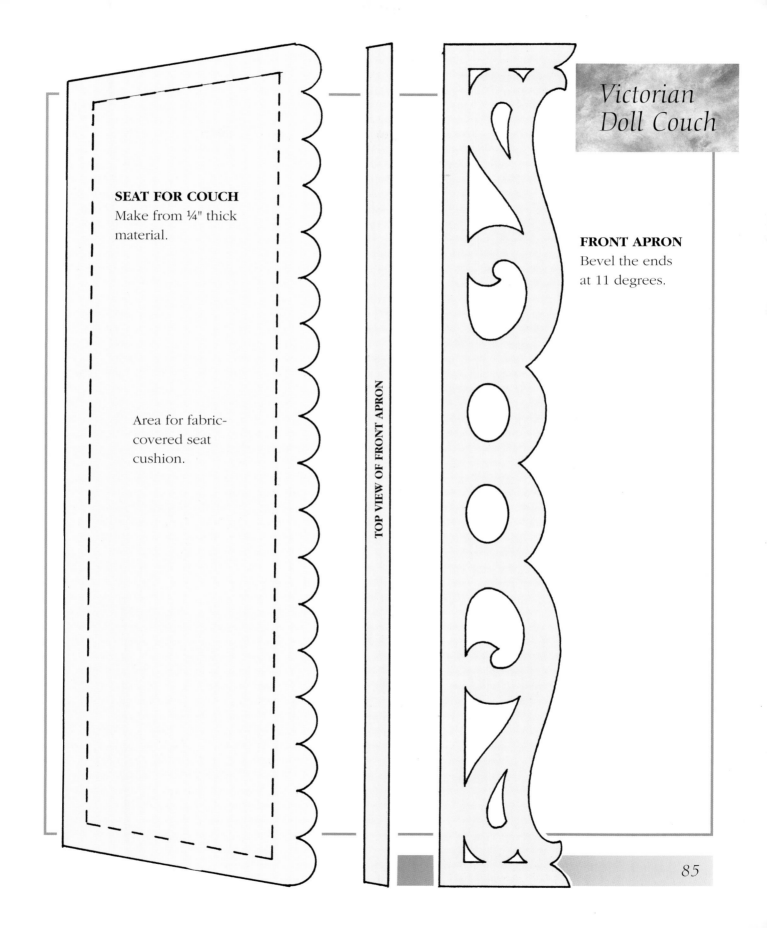

SEAT FOR COUCH
Make from ¼" thick material.

Area for fabric-covered seat cushion.

TOP VIEW OF FRONT APRON

Victorian Doll Couch

FRONT APRON
Bevel the ends at 11 degrees.

85

Victorian Doll Table

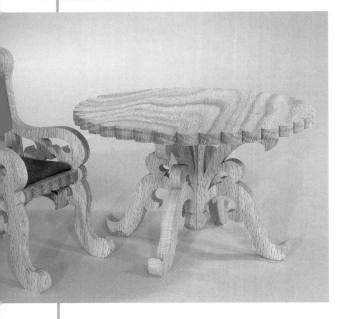

TABLETOP
Make from ¼" thick material.

(Make 2 copies of the pattern
and join them along centerline.)

CL

TABLE LEGS
Make from ¼" thick material.
Join along the halved-joint.

(Adjust the width of the joint to fit.)

10

DECORATIVE SCROLL SIGNAGE

The Boelman's house sign.

NOTE: You may want to enlarge the patterns to accommodate long names. You can also reduce or enlarge the alphabet on page 92 to fit.

HOW TO MAKE YOUR HOUSE SIGN

Make 2 copies of the pattern on this page, and join the dotted lines together to make the full-size pattern to produce the ornamental background for the sign. (See the illustration on page 91.)

Make 2 copies of this pattern, and join them together on the dotted lines to produce the full-size pattern for the overlay. (See illustration on page 91.)

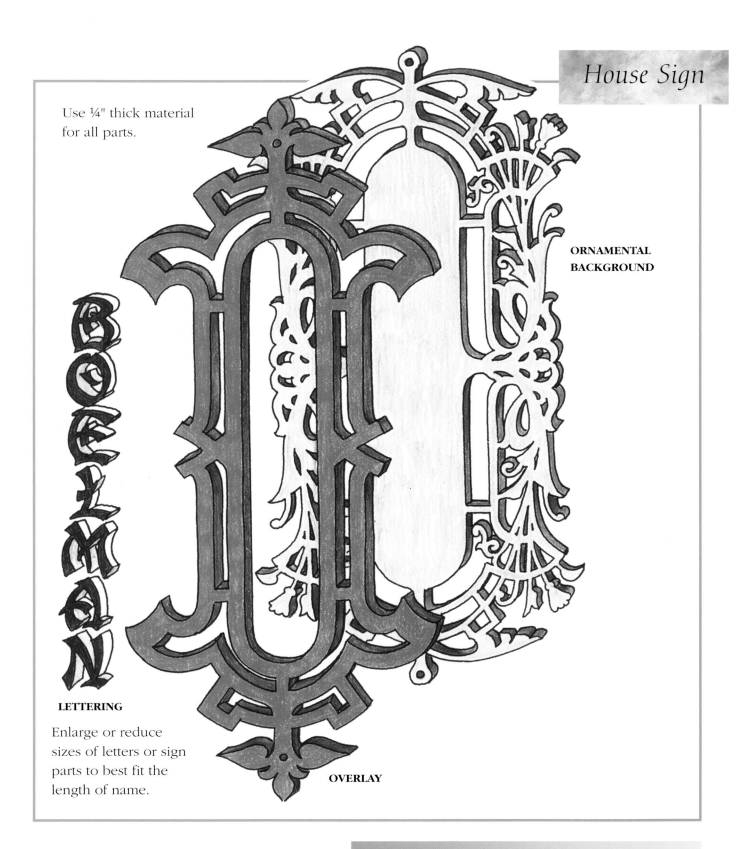

Use ¼" thick material for all parts.

ORNAMENTAL BACKGROUND

BORHMAN

LETTERING

Enlarge or reduce sizes of letters or sign parts to best fit the length of name.

OVERLAY

USE THESE NUMBERS TO UPDATE 1ST CHRISTMAS ORNAMENT

1234567890

ABCDE
FGHIJK
LMNOPQ
RSTUV
WXYZ

Update the year for this ornament with number patterns found on the opposite page.

A

B

A

B

You may want to enlarge the patterns by 115 percent on a photocopy machine to bring the design to full size.

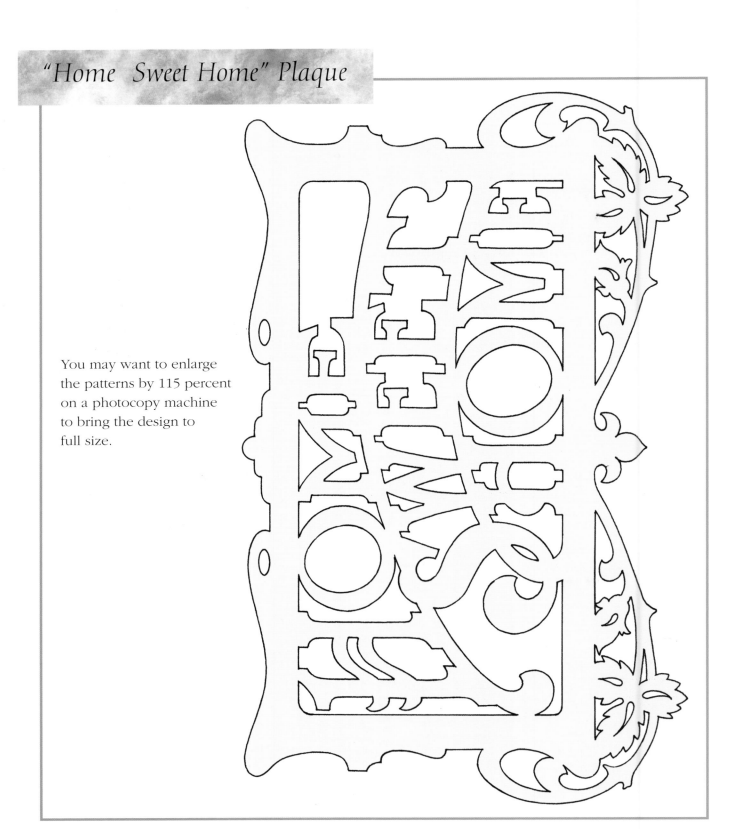

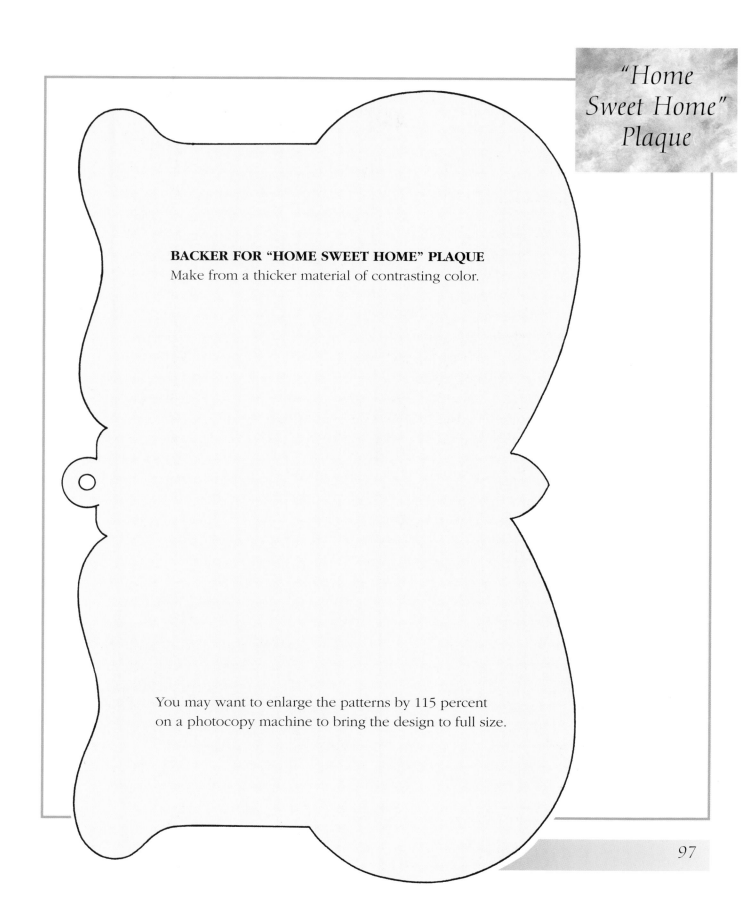

BACKER FOR "HOME SWEET HOME" PLAQUE
Make from a thicker material of contrasting color.

You may want to enlarge the patterns by 115 percent
on a photocopy machine to bring the design to full size.

Make from ¾" thick material.

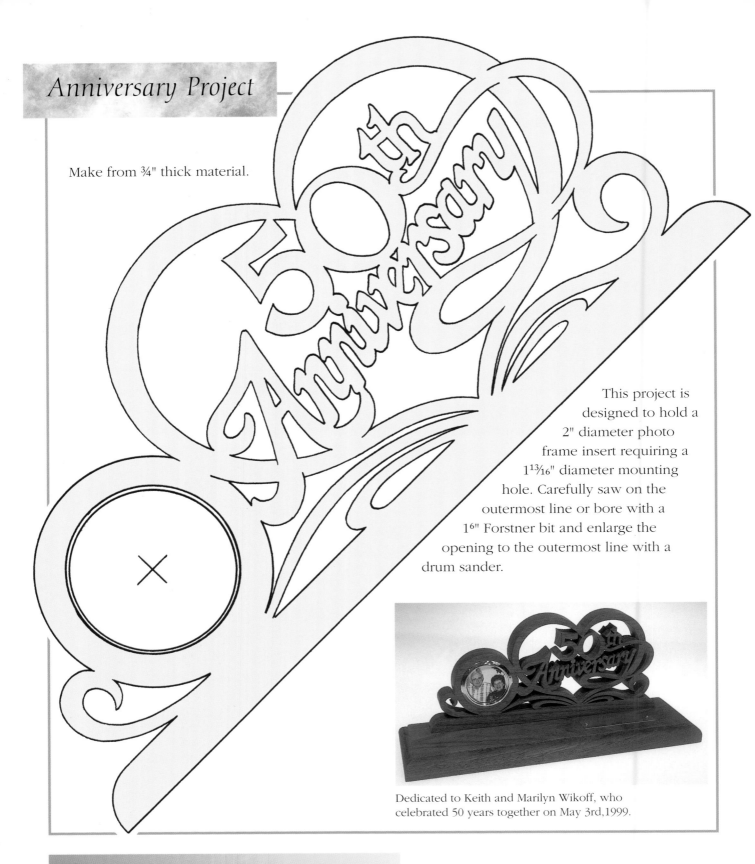

This project is designed to hold a 2" diameter photo frame insert requiring a 1¹³⁄₁₆" diameter mounting hole. Carefully saw on the outermost line or bore with a 1⁶" Forstner bit and enlarge the opening to the outermost line with a drum sander.

Dedicated to Keith and Marilyn Wikoff, who celebrated 50 years together on May 3rd, 1999.

NUMBERS & LETTERS. Use these to modify the pattern as needed: 1st, 25th, 33rd, 40th, 82nd, or whatever.

1 2 3 4 6 7 8

st nd rd

OPTIONAL

Add a ¾" x 3" or 1" x 4" brass plaque with names and date.

TOP VIEW OF BASE. Shown half size. Make base from ¾" thick material.

¾"

3½"

UPRIGHT

No. 6 x 1" flathead wood screws.   Bevel or shape edges as desired.

FRONT VIEW

1¼"   1¼"

11¼"

Tying-the-Knot

A gorgeous gift to make and give to newlyweds, and for wedding anniversaries, too! Use the following patterns to create names, dates, and decorative elements for the project. Then follow the instructions to make a backer board to mount all of the parts onto.

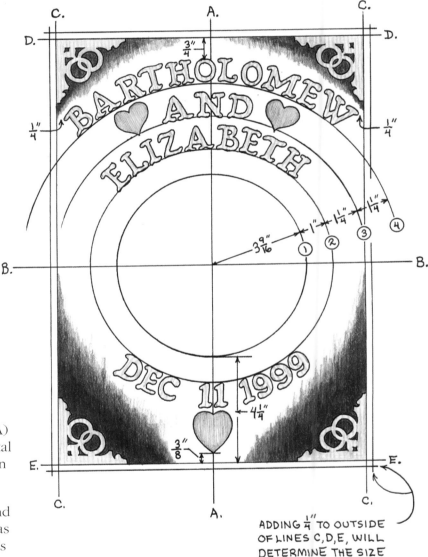

ADDING ¼" TO OUTSIDE OF LINES C, D, E, WILL DETERMINE THE SIZE OF THE BACKERBOARD.

DETERMINING THE SIZE OF THE BACKER BOARD

- Get a large sheet of paper, approx. 17" x 22". (Or tape smaller sheets together as needed.)

- On the paper, draw a vertical line (A–A) down the center. Also draw a horizontal line (B–B) to create the center point on the paper.

- Place a compass at the center point, and draw a 7⅛" diameter circle, indicated as (1) at the right, with a 3⁹⁄₁₆" radius. This is the mounting area for the large decorative circle.

- Extend the compass 1" to draw another circle (2). Use this circle as your guide to place the names above the circles, and dates below it, as shown in the illustration on the opposite page.

- Short names like "Dirk & Karen" will fit on one line, but you will need additional circles/lines for longer names such as "Bartholomew and Elizabeth," or to include last names. Extend the compass an additional 1¼" for each line, as indicated by circles (3) and (4).

- After placing the names and dates in proper locations (centers on the line A–A), determine placements for the corner brackets: Measure the widest portion of your project (e.g., Bartholomew); add a minimum ¼ beyond each end, and mark to produce two vertical lines (C–C).

- From the top edge of the topmost line of letters, add ¾", and draw a horizontal line (D–D).

- Measure down 4¼" below circle (1); draw horizontal line (E–E).

- Place the large heart ⅜" above line (E–E), and position the four brackets in the corners produced by the lines (C–C, D–D, E–E).

- Finally, add a line ¼" beyond the lines (C–C, D–D, E–E) to define the size of the backer board. (This ¼" space fits inside rabbet of lip of the frame.)

AT THIS POINT, OBSERVE COMPLETED LAYOUT AND MAKE ADJUSTMENTS AS DESIRED
. . . then measure and cut the backer board from ¼" thick material.

PLANNING THE FRAME

- To determine the quantity of material you need for your frame: Measure the width and length of your backer board; add 2" to each dimension, and then double that number. For example: Assume your backer board is 10" x 14¼" as shown to the right. Add 2" to each dimension, making them 12" and 16½". Double these numbers, which equals 24" and 33". Just add these together for a total of 57" of framing material needed.

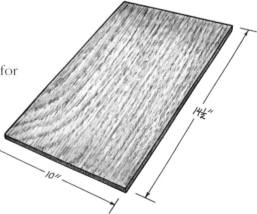

BACKER BOARD. 10" x 14½"

MAKING THE FRAME . . .

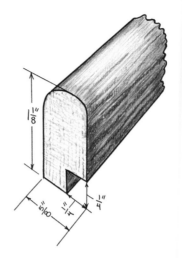

- The frame is made from ⅝" x 1⅛" material. On the bottom edge, use a router and bit to create a rabbet or lip ¼" wide by ¼" deep. Use a round-over bit to shape the top edge as shown to the right.

CUTTING FRAME PIECES TO SIZE

- Once again, refer to the dimensions of your backer board. Add 1¾" to both dimensions. (For example, using our backer board illustrated on page 101, which is 10" x 14½", 10" + 1¾" = 11¾", and 14½" + 1¾" = 16¼".) You will need two pieces cut at each length you determine for your project. Miter both ends of each piece at 45 degrees.

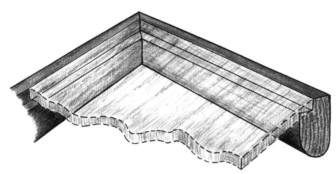

- Test-fit the frame pieces around the backer board and adjust to fit. (See the drawing to the left where the backer board is shown with dashed lines.) Use glue to fasten corners of the frame. Clamp together until dry. Small brads can also be used to secure joints if desired.

- Next, lay all the parts in their proper positions on the backer board. Remove one part at a time; apply glue to back side; and reposition onto backer board. (Do not glue the corner brackets in place until the frame has been attached to the backer board.) Before gluing the birds on, attach a length of cord or string to the heart, and wrap to form a knot-like area between the birds' beaks.

- Attach backer board to frame. This can be installed permanently with glue and brads, or temporarily with clips or cleats.

- Glue the corner brackets in place . . . attach a hanger to the backside . . . and **ENJOY!!**

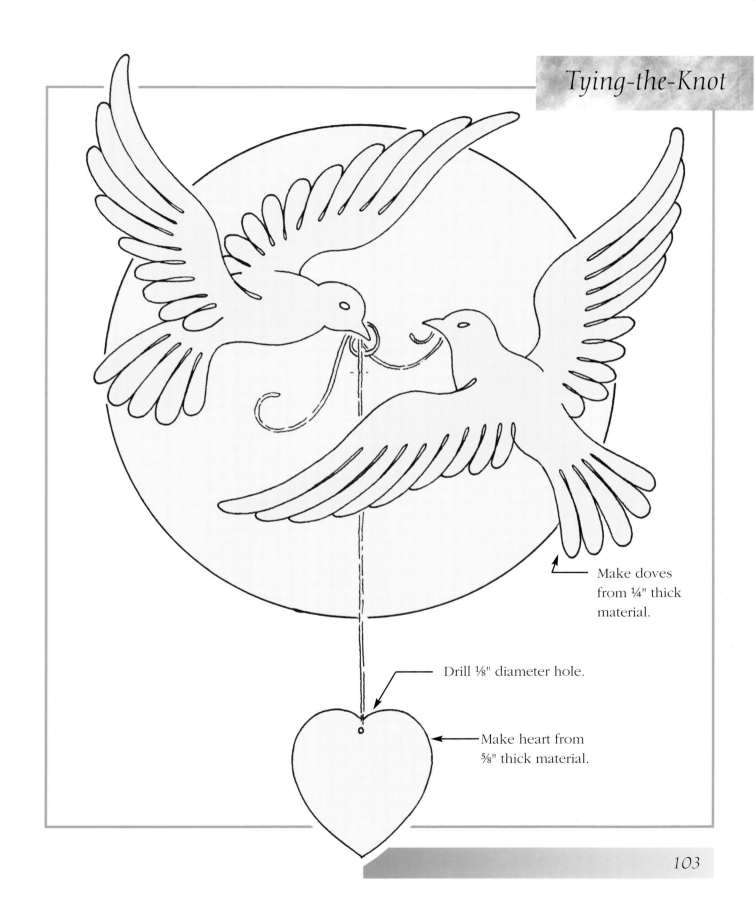

Make doves
from ¼" thick
material.

Drill ⅛" diameter hole.

Make heart from
⅝" thick material.

103

Make from ½"
thick material.

ABCD
EFGHI
JKLMNO
PQRSTU
VWXYZ
&1234567
890$¢:? ♥

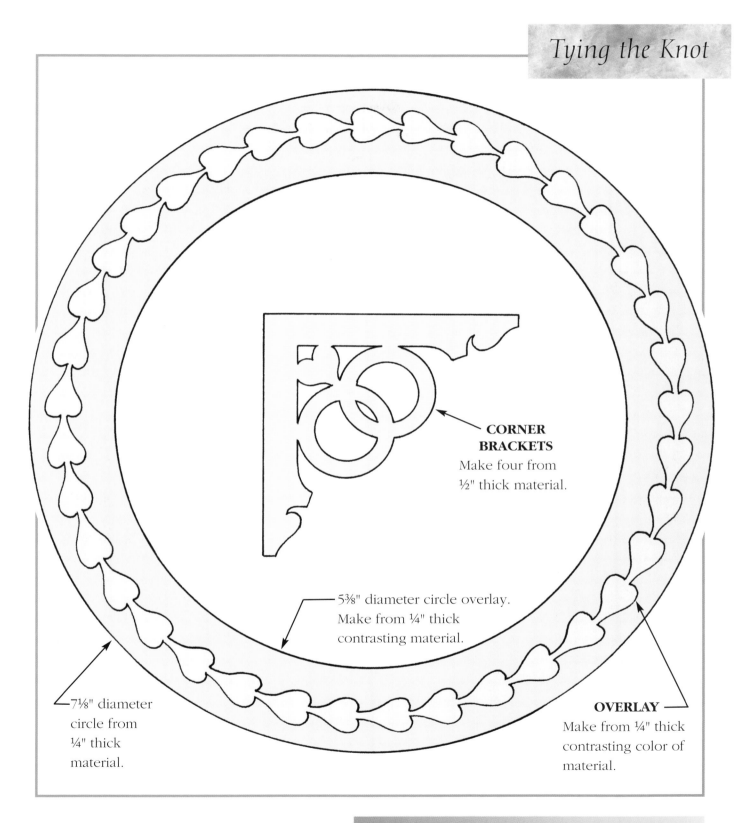

CORNER BRACKETS
Make four from ½" thick material.

5⅜" diameter circle overlay. Make from ¼" thick contrasting material.

7⅛" diameter circle from ¼" thick material.

OVERLAY
Make from ¼" thick contrasting color of material.

11

JEWELRY

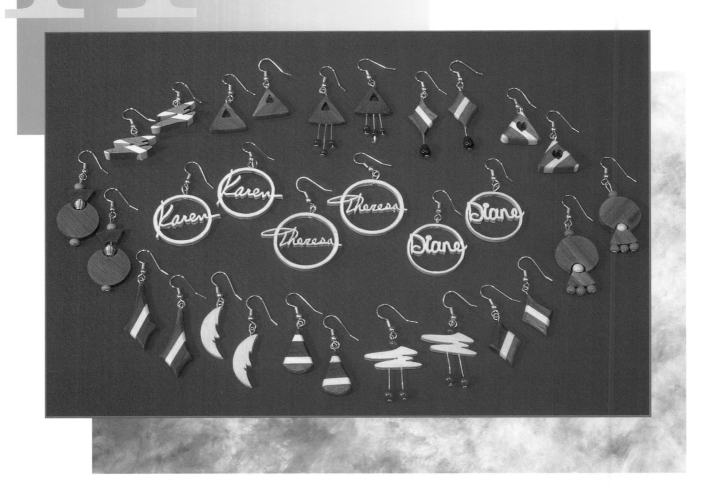

Use the patterns to create stunning earrings such as these, or simply make a circle border around a signature, and cut out with your scroll saw to produce "signature earrings."

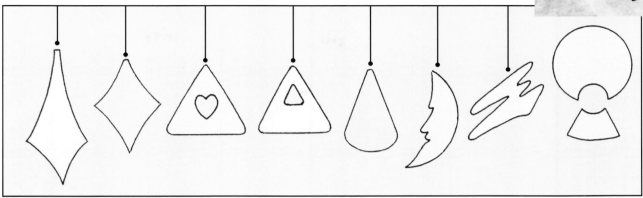

You can make these **EARRINGS** from your favorite colors of domestic and exotic hardwoods . . . or stain or paint them!

ANOTHER FUN WAY TO MAKE THE EARRINGS

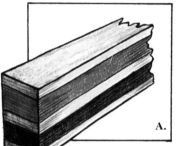

- Stack up and glue together thin strips of contrasting colors of wood (see **A**). Use various thicknesses of wood for optimum results.

- Be sure to spread glue evenly over the entire surface of each strip of wood. Clamp together and allow glue to set-up overnight.

- After glue dries, slice off ⅛" to ¼" thick slabs of the multi-layered material (see **B**).

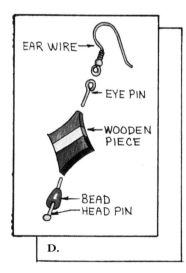

- Use spray glue to temporarily adhere the patterns to the wood at an angle as shown in **C**. After cutting out the wooden designs, decide upon location of the ear wires, beads, and pins (see **D**).

- Use a No. 70 drill bit to make small holes in the wooden pieces to accept the eye and head pins. The pins should extend a minimum of ⅛" into the wood (more is better).

- After drilling the holes, shape the edges of wooden pieces as desired, and polish smooth. Apply finish as desired.

- The eye and head pins are approx. 2" long when purchased. Trim to desired length with wire cutters.

- Put beads onto the head pins as desired.

- Insert pins into the holes in wooden pieces. Secure with glue if too loose.

The 5 basic components for creating these earrings

12 DECORATIVE HOME ACCESSORIES

Gargoyle book rack.

Make from ½" or ¾" thick material.

Make from ¼" thick material.

OVERLAY FOR FRAME

Make the overlay for the frame
from ⅛" thick material, perhaps
of a contrasting color.

The overlay will create a lip, or
rabbet, to hold the photo or
the mirror in place.

Use this pattern to trim photos
or mirrors to fit inside the frame.

It can also be used to produce
cardboard backing to install
behind photos.

Scissors Holder

A - B

Join the pattern sections along line (A-B).

Cut the whole pattern from ¼" thick material.

Make two **SPACERS** ½" x ⅝" x 3½", and glue in position shown.

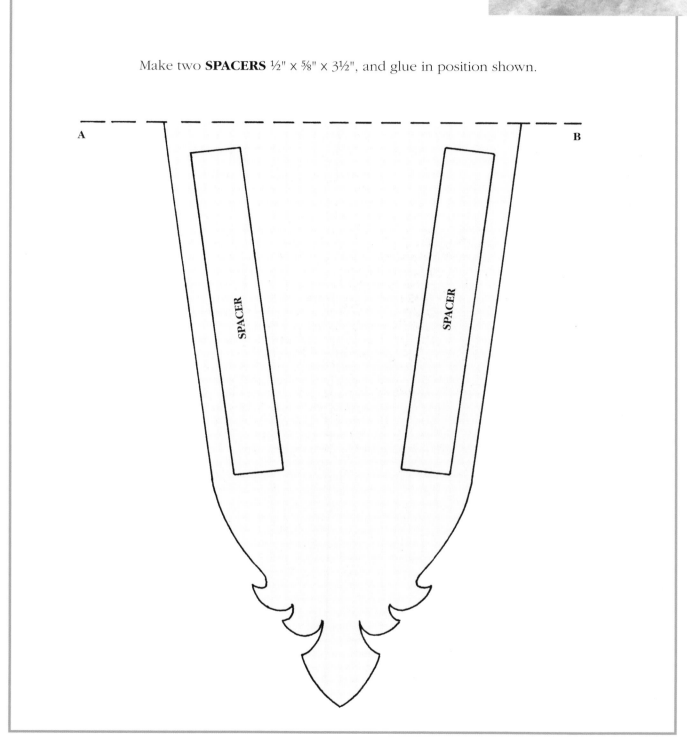

A   SPACER   SPACER   B

FRONT PANEL

Make from ¼" thick material.

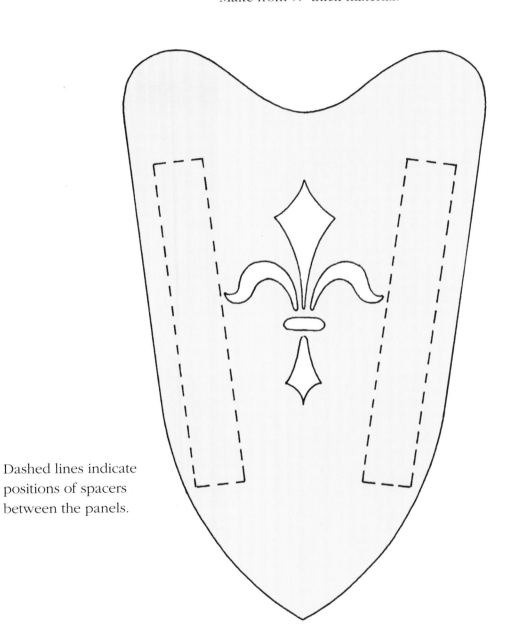

Dashed lines indicate
positions of spacers
between the panels.

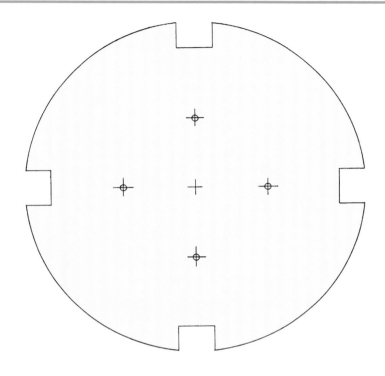

BOTTOM PANEL

Enlarge the pattern 200 percent.

Make from ¾" thick material. Adjust widths of joint areas as needed.

Predrill holes for screws to attach the base to uprights.

When you are ready to assemble all of the pieces, attach the base with glue and wood screws.

Enlarge pattern 200 percent on a photocopy machine.

Make from ¾" thick material.

Adjust width of joint area, as needed, to match the actual thickness of the material you will be using. (Lay your material on edge directly on the pattern, and trace the outline; saw slightly to the inside edge of your newly drawn pattern lines; sand or file to fit.)

JOINT AREA

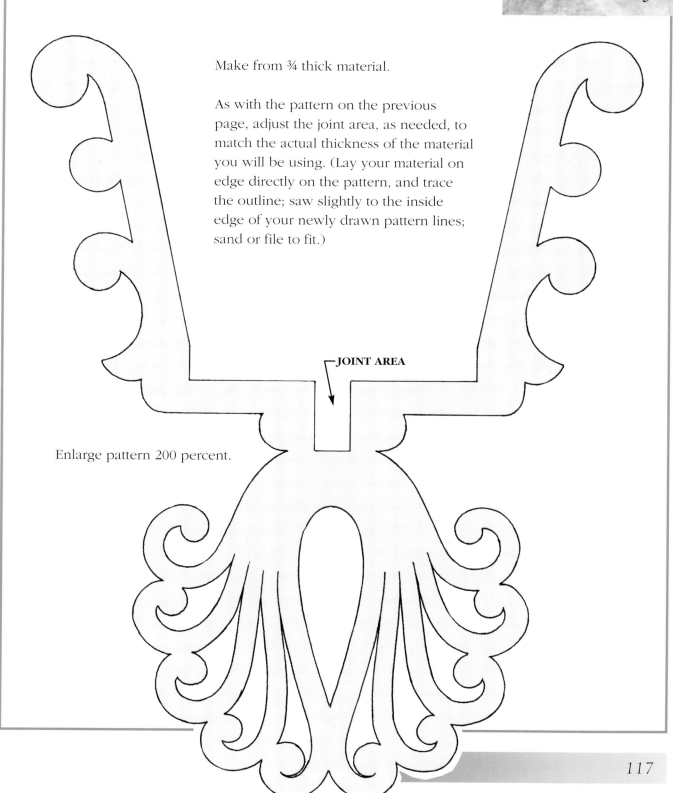

Make from ¾ thick material.

As with the pattern on the previous page, adjust the joint area, as needed, to match the actual thickness of the material you will be using. (Lay your material on edge directly on the pattern, and trace the outline; saw slightly to the inside edge of your newly drawn pattern lines; sand or file to fit.)

JOINT AREA

Enlarge pattern 200 percent.

Victorian Wall Shelf

**SHELF SUPPORT
BRACKET**
Make from
¼" thick
material.

SHELF
Make from ¼" thick material.

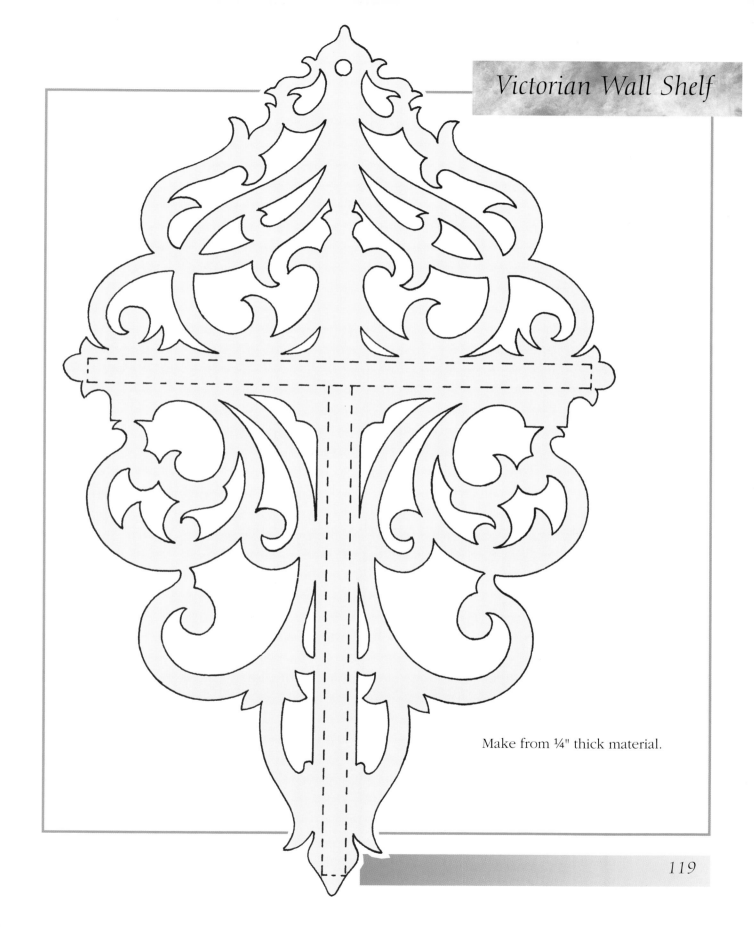

Make from ¼" thick material.

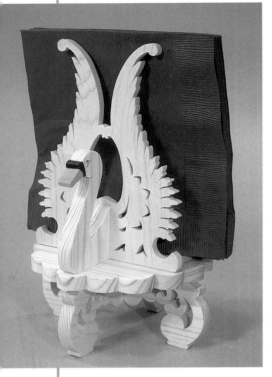

WINGS

Make 2 from ¼" thick material.

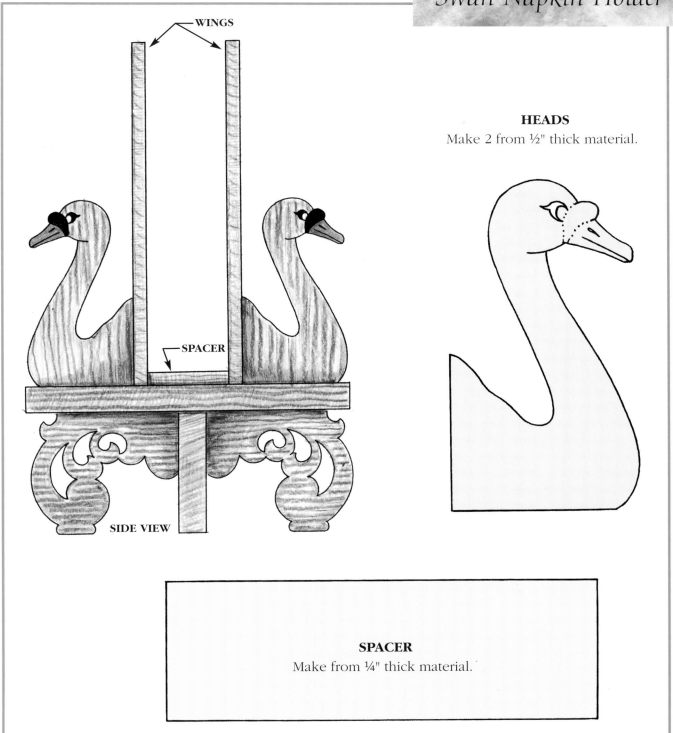

WINGS

SIDE VIEW

SPACER

HEADS
Make 2 from ½" thick material.

SPACER
Make from ¼" thick material.

Swan Napkin Holder

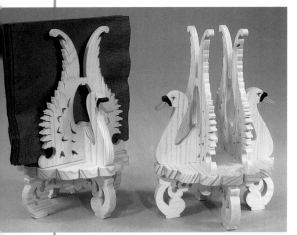

LEGS

Make from ½" thick material. Since thicknesses of most materials vary, adjust the width of the half-joint to match the material you are using. (Lay your material on edge directly on the pattern, and trace the outline; saw slightly to the inside edge of your newly drawn pattern lines; sand or file to fit.)

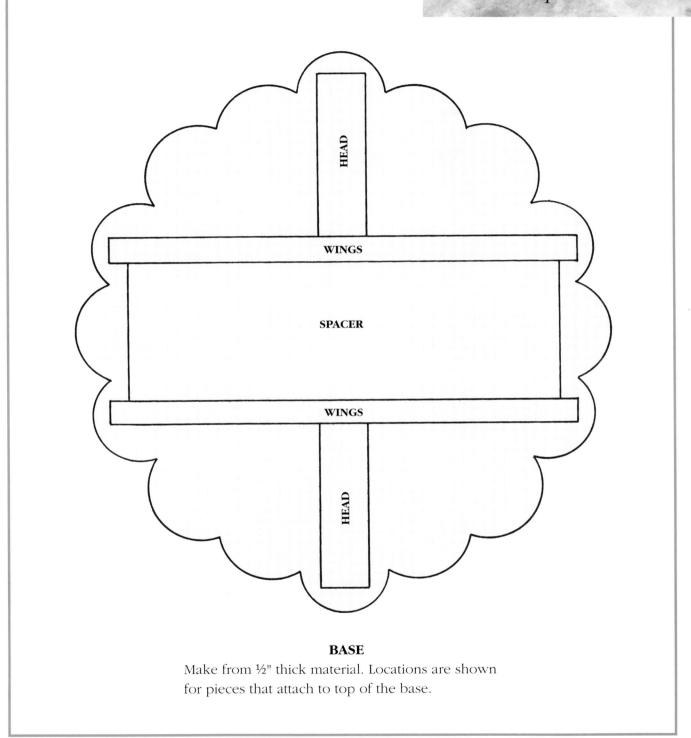

BASE

Make from ½" thick material. Locations are shown
for pieces that attach to top of the base.

Gargoyle Book Rack

Make 2 upright pieces from ½" thick material.

Bore ⁹⁄₆₄" diameter holes for two No. 6 x 1" screws to attach uprights to ends of the shelf.

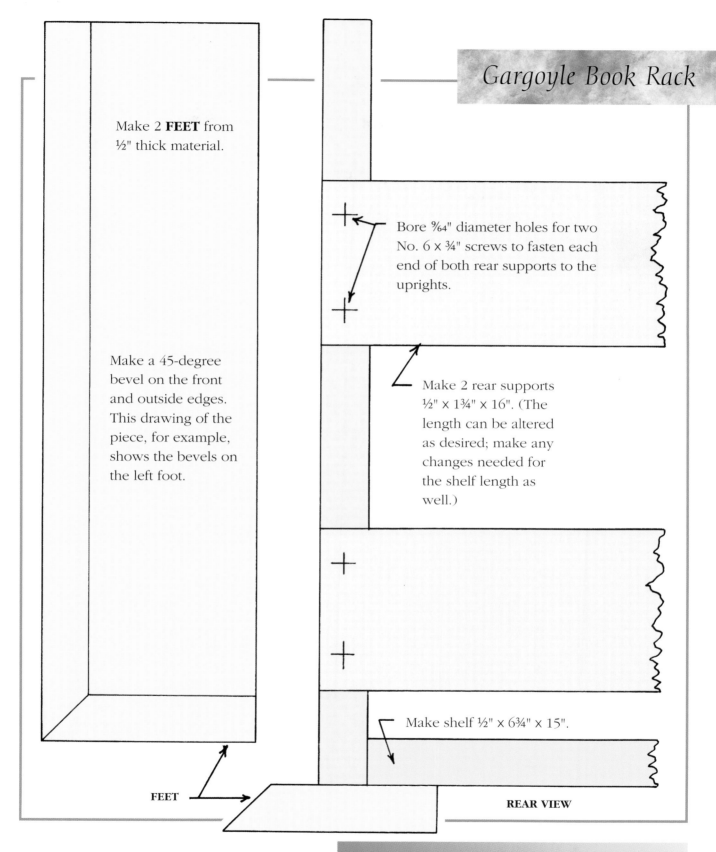

Make 2 **FEET** from ½" thick material.

Make a 45-degree bevel on the front and outside edges. This drawing of the piece, for example, shows the bevels on the left foot.

Bore %4" diameter holes for two No. 6 x ¾" screws to fasten each end of both rear supports to the uprights.

Make 2 rear supports ½" x 1¾" x 16". (The length can be altered as desired; make any changes needed for the shelf length as well.)

Make shelf ½" x 6¾" x 15".

FEET

REAR VIEW

METRIC CONVERSION

<table>
<tr><th colspan="3">Feet and Inch Conversions</th></tr>
<tr><td>1 inch</td><td>=</td><td>25.4 millimeters</td></tr>
<tr><td>1 foot</td><td>=</td><td>304.8 millimeters</td></tr>
</table>

<table>
<tr><th colspan="3">Metric Conversions</th></tr>
<tr><td>1 millimeter</td><td>=</td><td>0.039 inches</td></tr>
<tr><td>1 meter</td><td>=</td><td>3.28 feet</td></tr>
</table>

Inches to Millimeters and Centimeters

mm—millimeter   cm—centimeter

inches	mm	cm	inches	mm	cm	inches	mm	cm
⅛	3	0.3	3	76	7.6	12	305	30.5
¼	6	0.6	3½	89	8.9	13	330	33.0
⅜	10	1.0	4	102	10.2	14	356	35.6
½	13	1.3	4½	114	11.4	15	381	38.1
⅝	16	1.6	5	127	12.7	16	406	40.6
¾	19	1.9	5½	140	14.0	17	432	43.2
⅞	22	2.2	6	152	15.2	18	457	45.7
1	25	2.5	6½	165	16.5	19	483	48.3
1¼	32	3.2	7	178	17.8	20	508	50.8
1½	38	3.8	8	203	20.3	21	533	53.3
1¾	44	4.4	9	229	22.9	22	559	55.9
2	51	5.1	10	254	25.4	23	584	58.4
2½	64	6.4	11	279	27.9	24	610	61.0

Index

About the Authors

Dirk Boelman has been designing and drawing patterns since the early 1980s, when the resurgence in the popularity of scroll sawing began. He has produced thousands of patterns that have appeared in countless books, magazines, and other publications. Dirk publishes a newsletter *Scroll Saw Chatter*, and sells patterns and supplies through his own mail-order catalog.

Dirk's ancestors were woodworkers, carpenters, and boatbuilders. An artitst in several mediums, he had an earlier career as a graphic artist in the advertising and commercial printing industry. Dubbing himself as "The Art Factory," he considers himself very fortunate to have made a business from his love to draw, paint, design, and create. It brings him great pleasure to share his artistic skills to help others experience the pride and satisfaction of creating beauty with their own hands.

Patrick Spielman lives surrounded by a hardwood forest in the famous tourist area of Door County in northeast Wisconsin. After college he taught high school and vocational woodworking for 27 years. Patrick left the classroom more than 10 years ago, but he continues to teach and share ideas and designs through his published works. He serves as a technical consultant and designer for a major tool manufacturer and enjoys lending his knowledge of woodworking to promote talent and activites of other artisans.

He has written more than 60 woodworking books. One of Patrick's proudest accomplishments is his book, *The Router Handbook,* which sold more than 1.5 million copies worldwide. His updated version, *The New Router Handbook,* was selected the best how-to book of 1994 by the National Association of Home and Workshop writers.